THE ART OF CREATIVE REAL ESTATE INVESTING

Key Expert Strategies in Flipping Techniques, Alternative Financing, Legal Tax Advantages & Risk-Free Rental Properties to Achieve Financial Freedom

HVNLY PUBLISHING

TABLE OF CONTENTS

INTRODUCTION

The realization that anyone can turn a small investment into a substantial real estate portfolio with the right strategies is transformative. This moment happened for us years ago and changed everything. We're not just talking about buying properties; we're talking about creative real estate investing. Here, innovative financing, house flipping, rental portfolio growth, and tax strategies help build wealth.

This book aims to empower you with this knowledge and understanding in a clear and straightforward way so that it is accessible and actionable for you, regardless of your financial starting point. Packed with practical strategies, real-life examples, and step-by-step instructions, you'll be prepared to embark on your journey to financial freedom through real estate.

Our own journey into real estate investing began with little experience but a strong desire for financial independence. Through learning, failures, and successes, we've developed creative strategies that have taken us from novice investors to a position of economic strength. By sharing our experiences, we hope to inspire you and show that success in real estate is attainable through persistence, resilience, and a willingness to learn.

Unlike other real estate books, this one is grounded in the latest data and firsthand experience, offering a more comprehensive look at investment strategies. Whether you're interested in traditional buy-and-hold properties, flipping houses, or mastering the BRRRR method, this book is filled with valuable insights for everyone.

Designed to be inclusive, this book caters to both financially constrained and affluent individuals who are looking to diversify, regardless of age, employment status, or location.

Each section of this book builds on the last, starting with foundational knowledge and taking you through advanced investment strategies. Not only will you learn about creative real estate investing, but you'll also gain access to practical tools, templates, and digital resources, which are listed in the back of the book.

As you read on, consider this a call to adopt the mindset of a successful real estate investor. With the insights and strategies provided, you can start building your path to wealth through real estate. Remember, this journey is about taking action, making informed decisions, and learning from every outcome.

We've dedicated the last chapter to sharing our personal experiences. We cover the beginning of a mutually beneficial friendship, our dive into the world of real estate investing in 2007, and what it took to build our rental portfolio. We also detail how we started renovating houses to flip years later and how the two strategies were combined to accelerate risk-free wealth-building. We hope our story will help you decide what best resonates with you.

We encourage you to share your stories and successes as you apply these strategies in your investment exploration. Together, we can achieve more than we ever thought possible. Let's embark on this journey together!

THE ESSENTIALS OF REAL ESTATE INVESTING AND BEYOND

Mastering the language of real estate is critical. It's like learning a new dialect, unlocking doors to opportunities while avoiding pitfalls. This chapter, especially if you are starting, is your toolkit, providing essential knowledge to navigate real estate investing confidently and effectively.

DECIPHERING REAL ESTATE TERMS: A GLOSSARY FOR BEGINNERS

Defining Key Terms

Real estate industry terminology can be intimidating, but understanding key concepts like equity, leverage, and liquidity is essential for making informed investment decisions. Equity, for example, represents your ownership stake in a property and is calculated as the property's value minus any outstanding mortgage. It's a crucial indicator of your investment's health.

Leverage involves using borrowed money, like a mortgage, to increase your potential returns. It lets you control a more significant asset with a smaller initial investment, amplifying gains and losses.

Liquidity, on the other hand, refers to how easily you can convert your real estate investment into cash. Properties with high liquidity can be sold quickly without significantly affecting their market value. This flexibility is valuable, especially in uncertain economic times or when you need capital for new opportunities.

Additional Common Terms

- Appreciation: The increase in the value of a property over time
- After Repair Value (ARV): The estimated value of a property after completed renovations, not in its current condition.
- BRRRR Method: This stands for Buy, Rehab, Rent, Refinance, and Repeat — a popular investment strategy.
- Comparative Market Analysis (CMA): An estimate of a home's price used to help sellers set listing prices and help buyers make competitive offers.
- Due Diligence: The comprehensive appraisal of a business or property before signing a contract.
- Fair Market Value (FMV): Is *the price of an asset when the buyer and seller have reasonable knowledge of it and are* willing to trade without pressure.
- Fix-and-Flip: The strategy of purchasing, renovating, and selling properties for a profit.
- Foreclosure: A process that's triggered when a homeowner fails to make their mortgage payments. When a home is foreclosed on, a lender typically repossesses the property and attempts to sell it to recover their loss.

- Hard Money Loan: A short-term loan from private investors or companies at higher interest rates used for investing.
- House Hacking: Buying a multifamily property, living in one unit, and renting out the others. It also applies to renting individual rooms in a single-family dwelling.
- Owner-Financed: A transaction in which a property's seller finances the purchase directly with the person or entity buying it, either in whole or in part.
- PITI (principal, interest, taxes & insurance): The four essential elements of a monthly mortgage payment
- REIT (Real Estate Investment Trust): A company that owns, operates, or finances income-producing real estate.
- Rent-to-Own: A deal in which you commit to renting a property for a specific period, with the option of buying it before the lease runs out.
- Subject-To: Acquiring property subject to the existing mortgage.
- Multifamily Syndications: A group of investors pools together their money to purchase an apartment building together.
- Wholesaling: Contracting a home with a seller, then finding an interested party to buy it for more.
- Wraparound Mortgage: This type of junior loan wraps or includes the current note due on the property. The wraparound loan will consist of the balance of the original loan plus an amount to cover the new purchase price for the property.

UNDERSTANDING PROPERTY TYPES

When investing in real estate, it is important to understand the various property types and their investment implications. Residential properties, ranging from single-family homes to multi-unit apartments, offer rental income and capital appreciation opportunities. However, they also require you to follow tenant laws and take charge of property maintenance.

Commercial properties, including office spaces, retail stores, storage, and warehouses, can yield higher rental income but demand a thorough analysis of business trends and economic cycles. Industrial real estate, such as factories and production facilities, often provides stable income through long-term leases, though it requires substantial investment and management. Land investments offer the potential for significant appreciation, but they require patience and a deep understanding of zoning laws and development possibilities.

Each property type comes with its own set of risks, rewards, and management strategies. Therefore, aligning your investment decisions with your financial objectives, risk tolerance, and ability to manage the property effectively is essential.

Real Estate Metrics Explained

The metrics and calculations that evaluate a property's performance and overall financial health are crucial for making smart investment choices. Let's break down what these metrics typically represent and why they are important:

- Net Operating Income (NOI): This is the total income generated from the property minus the operating expenses. It does not include mortgage payments, taxes, or insurance. NOI helps investors understand how much profit the property generates from its operations.

- Cap Rate (Capitalization Rate): This is calculated by dividing the NOI by the property's current market value. It measures the rate of return on a real estate investment. A higher cap rate indicates a higher return on investment, which can be attractive to investors.

- Cash Flow: This represents the amount of money left after all expenses, including mortgage payments, have been paid. Positive cash flow means the property generates more income than it costs to maintain, which is essential for the sustainability of the investment.

- Cash on Cash Return: This metric measures the return on the actual money invested in the property. It's calculated by dividing the annual pre-tax cash flow by the total cash invested. It helps investors understand the efficiency of their invested capital.

- Gross Rent Multiplier (GRM): This is the ratio of the property's price to its gross rental income. It's a quick way to estimate a property's value based on its rental income. A lower GRM suggests a better investment.

- Operating Expense Ratio (OER): This is the ratio of operating expenses to gross operating income. It helps understand how efficiently the property is being managed. A lower OER indicates higher efficiency.

- Debt Service Coverage Ratio (DSCR): This measures the property's ability to cover its debts with its NOI. It's calculated by dividing the NOI by the total debt service. A DSCR greater than 1 indicates the property generates sufficient income to cover its debt payments.

Contract Language Simplified

Real estate contracts outline in detail the agreements between parties, specifying rights, responsibilities, and contingencies. Clear and precise contract language prevents misunderstandings and safeguards your interests.

Important clauses include property descriptions, purchase prices, payment terms, contingencies like financing and inspections, and closing details such as dates and costs. Understanding these ensures you enter agreements fully aware of your obligations and the protections you have.

This chapter goes beyond introducing terms and aims to help you approach real estate investments thoughtfully and strategically. Understanding complex real estate terminology, property types, and key metrics lays the foundation for your entry into real estate investing. Understanding these concepts will change how you evaluate opportunities, negotiate deals, and make crucial investment decisions, allowing you to focus on investment options that match your strategy and financial goals.

EVALUATING YOUR FINANCIAL READINESS FOR REAL ESTATE INVESTING

A thorough and honest review of your financial health is crucial in real estate investing. This includes assessing assets, liabilities, and liquidity, as well as your financial habits and ability to sustain investments over time. It's essential to ensure you're staying within your budget. Being money-wise is critical; if you have not been good with your finances up to now, it is never too late to start.

For example, if you have been struggling with lingering and annoying credit card debt, consider the snowball effect to pay off balances. The snowball effect is a popular method for tackling credit card debt, where you focus on paying off the smallest debts first to build momentum and motivation. Here's a step-by-step guide to using the snowball effect to manage your credit card debt:

1. List Your Debts

Start by making a list of all your credit card debts. Include the balance, minimum monthly payment, and interest rate for each one. Order them from the smallest balance to the largest.

2. Make Minimum Payments on All Debts

Ensure you make at least the minimum payment on all your credit card debts every month. This will keep you in good standing with your creditors and avoid late fees and penalties.

3. Focus on the Smallest Debt

With the snowball method, you first concentrate on paying off the smallest debt. Any extra money you have after making the minimum payments should go toward this debt.

4. Pay Off the Smallest Debt

Put all your extra money toward the smallest debt until it's paid off completely. This gives you a quick win and a psychological boost.

5. Roll Over Payments to the Next Smallest Debt

Once the smallest debt is paid off, take the money you were putting toward that debt and add it to the minimum payment of the next smallest debt. Continue making the minimum payments on the other debts.

6. Repeat the Process

Continue this process, paying off each debt in order from smallest to largest. As you pay off each debt, the amount of money you can put toward the next debt grows, like a snowball rolling downhill and gaining size.

Here's an example to illustrate how the snowball effect works:

1. **Credit Card A:** $500 balance, $25 minimum payment.
2. **Credit Card B:** $1,500 balance, $50 minimum payment.
3. **Credit Card C:** $3,000 balance, $75 minimum payment.

Step-by-Step:

- **Step 1:** List your debts from smallest to largest (Credit Card A, B, C).
- **Step 2:** Make minimum payments on all three cards.
- **Step 3:** Focus any extra money on Credit Card A.

Suppose you have an extra $100 each month:

Pay the $25 minimum on Credit Card A plus the extra $100, totaling $125 monthly.
Continue making the minimum payments of $50 and $75 on Credit Cards B and C, respectively.

- **Step 4:** Once Credit Card A is paid off, move to Credit Card B.

Combine the $125 (previously going to Credit Card A) with the $50 minimum payment for Credit Card B. Now you're paying $175 per month on Credit Card B.
Continue making the $75 minimum payment on Credit Card C.

- **Step 5:** After Credit Card B is paid off, apply the $175 to Credit Card C, making your payment $250 per month until it's paid off.

BENEFITS OF THE SNOWBALL EFFECT

- **Motivation:** Quick wins keep you motivated.
- **Simplicity:** The method is straightforward and easy to follow.
- **Psychological Boost:** Paying off debts provides a sense of accomplishment and encourages continued progress.

Creditworthiness is key in real estate investing. A good credit score signals to lenders that you're reliable in repaying debts, potentially leading to better loan terms. Regular monitoring, timely payments, and strategic management of credit lines can help you maintain a solid credit score. Regularly monitoring your credit score is not an option; it is a must to succeed in real estate investing.

On a side note, something to consider is establishing credit under your company's name sooner rather than later. Creating a business entity for protection purposes is covered in Chapter 7, but it is worth mentioning that establishing a business also offers credit advantages. Charges made on business credit cards have no impact on your personal credit score. So, when you need to keep a balance on a credit card for more than one month, it is best to do so on a business credit card, safeguarding the health of your personal credit score.

Another thing to note is that while we stress the importance of having a good credit score, it is not necessary to start investing.

Many lenders overlook credit scores and only focus on the asset to approve a loan. We mentioned it because, in the long run, good credit will open more doors. Working on having the best credit score possible is worth the effort.

As you evaluate your financial readiness, risk management is crucial to ensuring success and involves identifying, assessing, and preventing potential financial hazards. This includes conducting thorough market analyses to understand local property values, rental demand, and economic indicators. Building a network of real estate professionals can also provide valuable insights and help address risks before they become problematic.

To create a profitable investment portfolio, you must manage all these financial elements in real estate investing. We know of many investors that conduct business in various markets across different states, and they do so successfully. Without a doubt, this has been possible by building a trustworthy team. It takes a village to get the job done effectively.

Now, let's stop and take a deep breath. If you are a novice in real estate investing and this overload of information is overwhelming you, keep your calm and continue reading. It will all make sense, little by little.

The Psychology Behind Successful Real Estate Investing

In the transformative world of real estate investing, success isn't just about physical properties; it's about mindset and emotions. Having a growth mindset, which sees challenges as opportunities to learn, is crucial. It helps investors bounce back from setbacks and apply learned lessons to future transactions with a clearer vision.

Decision-making in any realm requires analytical thinking and intuitive judgment. This is especially true when making decisions and being ready to pull the trigger in real estate deals. Cognitive strategies help investors analyze market trends and financial forecasts, balancing risks and rewards while avoiding biases that could cloud judgment.

Some examples of Cognitive Strategies:

1. **Heuristic Techniques:** Use simple, efficient rules of thumb for making frequent and quick real estate decisions. For example, the 1% rule for rental properties (a property should rent for 1% or more of its total upfront cost).
2. **Critical Thinking:** Apply skepticism and analysis. Investors should critically evaluate information, question assumptions, and analyze data before making decisions.
3. **Creative Visualization:** Use visualization techniques to imagine successful outcomes, plan renovation projects, or reconfigure the use of space in a property. This can enhance motivation and clarify the steps needed to achieve goals.
4. **Decision-Making Frameworks:** Create frameworks for making better investment decisions, such as SWOT analysis (Strengths, Weaknesses, Opportunities, Threats) or the DECIDE model (Define, Estimate, Consider, Identify, Decide, Evaluate).
5. **Mindfulness and Emotional Regulation:** Learn techniques to manage emotions and stress, which are crucial in high-stakes environments like real estate investing. Being able to stay calm under pressure can lead to more rational decision-making.

6. **Cognitive Restructuring:** Learn to identify and change negative thought patterns that could hinder investment success. For example, it is turning a fear of failure into an understanding that every setback is a learning opportunity.

7. **Problem-Solving Skills:** Develop advanced problem-solving skills, such as effectively tackling unexpected issues during property development or negotiating better deals.

8. **Learning from Mistakes:** Foster a mindset that views mistakes as learning opportunities. With a positive mindset, mistakes can lead to better methods or even unexpected success.

9. **Information Processing:** Work on the ability to process large amounts of information, which is crucial due to the complex and information-rich nature of real estate investing. This could include strategies for prioritizing information and quick recall techniques.

10. **Mental Modeling:** Construct mental models of the real estate market and investment processes. This helps visualize outcomes, understand complex transactions, and anticipate potential challenges.

Emotional intelligence involves understanding one's emotions and those of others, enabling effective communication and negotiation. This skill builds trust and strong client and collaborator relationships, which are vital for success.

The high-stress nature of real estate investing makes stress management essential. Practices like mindfulness and physical activity help manage stress, while time management and hobbies provide a much-needed break.

In real estate investing, success is not defined by financial gains but also by personal growth and development. While making money is important and undoubtedly needed, growing as a human being, and positively impacting others is priceless.

Common Myths vs. Realities

Real estate investment is often clouded by myths that can discourage both new and experienced investors. It is best to know the truth; this knowledge will empower you.

One common misconception is the get-rich-quick idea. This suggests that success happens overnight when the reality is that real estate investing requires hard work, diligence, and patience. It's a gradual process that requires consistent effort and strategic planning. Most often, this journey is not for the faint of heart.

Another common myth is the belief in no-money-down deals as a shortcut to real estate wealth. While these deals exist, they are complex and can be risky. They require a deep understanding of financial instruments and a solid contingency plan. However, we by no means discourage you from trying to find these deals; we simply advise you to be cautious and know what you are dealing with. One popular strategy used by investors getting started and who might have few assets or limited liquidity is to wholesale properties, which we'll get into a little later.

Among other tales, some investors believe they can perfectly time the market to maximize profits. Yet, the market is unpredictable, and success lies more in the quality of the investment and the investor's ability to adapt.

The narrative around risk and reward in real estate can also be misleading, often exaggerating rewards while downplaying risks.

Effective risk management is key here, and it involves diversification, thorough research, and cautious use of financial leverage.

By dispelling these myths and making informed decisions, investors can build a solid foundation for financial success in real estate, ensuring a legacy of wealth and wisdom for future generations.

THE IMPORTANCE OF ETHICAL INVESTING IN BUILDING LONG-TERM WEALTH

Focusing on profits in real estate investing can sometimes make us overlook our community impact. This can hinder sustainable growth and cause us to neglect our responsibility to uphold ethical standards in the industry. Ethical investing involves understanding that our investments impact others. It requires a thoughtful approach that balances financial goals with moral principles.

Building Trust with Ethical Practices

Trust is essential and is built through consistent ethical practices. Practices like transparency and fair treatment of tenants and clients lay the foundation for lasting relationships. Your reputation goes a long way and can help you attract clients, partners, and investors who prioritize honesty. However, this trust doesn't just benefit individuals; it also enhances the industry's credibility. Your reputation and ability to uphold ethical practices ensure long-term success, respect, and cooperation in real estate.

Reputation Management

Managing your reputation is a must in today's digital era. Ethical practices, once overlooked, are now closely watched by many, thanks to the transparency of social media and online platforms.

Any ethical misstep can quickly damage a reputation, while a commitment to ethics and sustainability can enhance it, setting you apart in the market. Once built and maintained, your reputation becomes an asset, opening doors to new partnerships, investments, and a loyal client base. But ethical investing isn't just about morals; it's a smart risk management strategy that, again, can help you stand out.

To build lasting wealth, you must integrate ethical practices into every investment decision. This approach defines success not just in financial terms but also in terms of community well-being. By focusing on trust and reputation, real estate investors can create environments where everyone thrives.

Identifying Your Real Estate Investing Goals

Setting clear, attainable investment goals starts with understanding your motivations. This includes your financial goals but also broader objectives like stable income, community impact, and personal milestones. Having clear goals guides your investment decisions and helps measure success.

In real estate, goals can vary from short-term to long-term. Short-term goals focus on quick financial gains, like wholesaling, flipping properties, or renovating rentals for higher rates. These can be lucrative but come with risks and require market insight. Long-term goals aim for asset value growth, equity accumulation, or passive rental income. Balancing these goals requires understanding market dynamics, financial health, risk tolerance, and time horizon.

To further explain time horizon, it refers to the period an investor expects to hold a property before selling it or achieving a particular financial goal. This duration can significantly influence the investment strategy, property selection, financing options, and risk management approach. Here's a breakdown of different time horizons in real estate investing:

1. Short-term Horizon (1-3 years):

- Strategy: Flipping properties or short-term rentals.
- Focus: Quick renovations and resales, capitalizing on market trends, or leveraging high-demand rental periods.
- Risks: Market volatility, higher transaction costs, and the potential for unexpected expenses during renovation.

2. Medium-term Horizon (3-7 years):

- Strategy: Buy-and-hold with a plan to sell aftermarket appreciation.
- Focus: Stabilizing rental income, moderate property improvements, and benefiting from property appreciation.
- Risks: Changes in market conditions and economic cycles that can affect property values.

3. Long-term Horizon (7+ years):

- Strategy: Buy-and-hold for long-term rental income and appreciation.
- Focus: Consistent rental income, property maintenance, and long-term appreciation.
- Risks: Economic downturns, changes in neighborhood dynamics, and long-term maintenance costs.

Measuring success in real estate goes beyond profits and includes metrics like return on investment and tenant satisfaction. Knowledge and market navigation skills are also success indicators. Real estate investing is about both money and personal growth.

The real estate market and your personal circumstances may change, so it's important to reassess and adjust goals regularly. This allows you to respond to market shifts and life changes. For example, you might shift from rental properties to flipping based on interest rates or personal needs. It is a common strategy for investors to do a few flips to generate enough income to buy a rental and keep it in their portfolio.

We have news for those who want to invest in real estate but do not envision yourself finding properties, tearing down walls for a flip, or overseeing people as they get the job done for you. Chapter 2 and Chapter 6 will cover various options for investing in real estate without ever stepping into a property.

FINDING DEALS SIMPLIFIED

Navigating the real estate market to find lucrative deals can be daunting, especially for new investors. However, the process becomes significantly more manageable with a strategic approach and the right tools. Start by leveraging online real estate platforms such as Zillow, Redfin, and Realtor.com to explore market listings and identify potential properties. Utilize public records and county websites to uncover distressed properties and foreclosure listings—partner with real estate agents and wholesalers who have access to off-market deals and valuable insights. Employ direct mail campaigns targeting absentee landlords and owners of distressed properties to create opportunities for negotiation. Combining these resources with thorough market research and networking allows you to streamline your search for real estate investments, making the process more efficient and effective.

REAL ESTATE AGENTS AND BROKERS

- **Network with Local Agents:** Build relationships with real estate agents who can access the Multiple Listing Service (MLS) and alert you to new listings.
- **Buyer's Agents:** Hire an agent who specializes in working with investors and understands your criteria.

Online Real Estate Marketplaces

- **MLS Listings:** Access through real estate agents or online platforms like Realtor.com, Zillow, and Redfin.
- **Auction Sites:** Websites like Auction.com and Hubzu offer properties up for auction, often below market value.

Foreclosure Listings

- **Bank Websites:** Many banks list their foreclosed properties on their websites.
- **Government Listings:** HUD, Fannie Mae, and Freddie Mac list foreclosed properties for sale on their respective websites.
- **Local Courthouse:** Attend foreclosure auctions at your local courthouse.

Real Estate Wholesalers

- **Networking:** Connect with wholesalers who specialize in finding off-market deals and selling them to investors at a markup.

- **Online Wholesaler Platforms:** Websites like Connected Investors and BiggerPockets have sections dedicated to wholesale deals.

Driving for Dollars

- **Neighborhood Exploration:** Drive through neighborhoods looking for distressed or vacant properties. Note the addresses and reach out to the owners.

NETWORKING EVENTS AND REAL ESTATE INVESTMENT GROUPS

- **Local Meetups:** Join local real estate investment groups and attend networking events to meet other investors and potential sellers.
- **Real Estate Clubs:** Participate in real estate investment clubs where members share deals and opportunities.

Online Classifieds and Marketplaces

- **Craigslist and Facebook Marketplace:** Look for properties listed for sale by owner (FSBO) and contact sellers directly.
- **Local Online Forums:** Join local real estate forums and social media groups where members post deals.

Public Records

- **Probate Sales:** Check public records for properties in probate, which may be available for purchase from heirs looking to sell quickly.
- **Divorce and Bankruptcy Records:** Properties involved in divorce or bankruptcy proceedings may be sold at a discount.

Real Estate Auctions

- **County Tax Sales:** Attend county tax lien and deed sales where properties with delinquent taxes are auctioned off.
- **Estate Sales:** Look for estate sales that include real estate properties.

Networking with Other Investors

- **Joint Ventures:** Partner with experienced investors who have access to deals but need capital or other resources you can provide.
- **Referrals:** Ask other investors for referrals to sellers looking to offload properties.

MARKETING AND ADVERTISING

Online Ads: Use Google Ads, Facebook Ads, and other online advertising platforms to target potential sellers.

Bandit Signs: Place signs in strategic locations with a simple message like "We Buy Houses for Cash" and a contact number.

Direct Mail Campaigns

- **Targeted Mailers:** Send postcards or letters to owners of distressed properties, absentee landlords, or those with significant equity who might be willing to sell.

A STEP-BY STEP GUIDE TO DIRECT MAIL CAMPAIGNS (NOT MEANT TO BE EXHAUSTIVE)

Identify Distressed Properties

- **Public Records:** Check local county websites or the county clerk's office for public records of properties in foreclosure, tax delinquency, or other financial distress.

  Example: Visit the official website of your county's recorder or assessor and search for foreclosure listings.

- **Foreclosure Listing Websites:** Use websites like RealtyTrac, Foreclosure.com, or Auction.com to find listings of distressed properties.

Locate Absentee Landlords

- **Property Tax Records:** Access property tax records to find properties where the owner's mailing address is different from the property address, indicating an absentee landlord.

  Example: Visit your local tax assessor's website and search for properties by mailing address.

- **Real Estate Data Services:** Use services like CoreLogic or PropertyRadar that offer detailed property and ownership data, including absentee landlords. A subscription is usually required.

Identify Properties with Significant Equity

- **Online Property Valuation Tools:** Using tools like Zillow, Redfin, or Realtor.com to estimate property values can often be misleading. It is best to have access to a CMA (Comparative Market Analysis) and compare them to outstanding mortgage balances.
- **Real Estate Data Services:** Services like CoreLogic or ATTOM Data Solutions provide comprehensive data, including mortgage balances and equity information.

Acquire Mailing Lists

- **Direct Mail Services:** Companies like Listsource, DirectMail.com, and InfoUSA offer targeted mailing lists for specific criteria, such as distressed properties, absentee landlords, or properties with high equity.

  Example: Visit ListSource to create and purchase a targeted mailing list.

Executing a successful direct mail campaign requires careful planning, execution, and follow-up to keep your readers engaged and prompt them to respond. Once you have defined your goals and target audience and developed your mailing list, you must carefully plan your next steps.

Craft Your Message

- Develop a compelling copy that clearly communicates your offer and includes a solid call to action (CTA).
- Design your mail piece (postcard, letter, brochure) with eye-catching graphics and a clean layout.

Offer and CTA

- Provide an enticing offer that adds value (solves a problem) and motivates the recipient to respond.
- Ensure the CTA (call to action) is clear, straightforward, and easy to follow.

Printing and Production

- Choose a reliable printer to produce high-quality mail pieces.
- Ensure all elements (envelopes, inserts, etc.) are ready for assembly.

Example: Use direct mail marketing services like Vistaprint, PostcardMania, or Yellow Letters Complete to design, print, and prepare your postcards or letters for sending.

Mailing Schedule

- Plan the timing of your mail-outs to align with your campaign goals and the recipient's behavior patterns.
- Consider staggering the mail-outs to manage response rates and follow-ups more effectively.

First Mail-Out

- Send out the first batch of mail pieces.
- Track delivery and ensure that your mail pieces are reaching the intended recipients.

Follow-Up Plan

- Plan a follow-up strategy, such as sending a reminder or additional information to recipients who did not respond to the first mail-out.

Track Responses

- Set up mechanisms to track responses (unique phone numbers, URLs, QR codes, response cards).
- Monitor response rates and gather data on recipient engagement.

Second Mail-Out

- Send a second mail piece to non-responders or as a reminder to all recipients.
- This piece should build on the initial message, reiterating the offer and CTA.

Engagement Tactics

- Incorporate personalized elements (recipient's name, specific offers) to increase engagement.
- Use multiple channels to engage (email, phone calls, text) alongside your direct mail.

Feedback Loop

- Collect feedback from respondents to understand their motivations and barriers.
- Use this information to refine your message and offer for future mail-outs.

Analyze Results

- Evaluate the effectiveness of your campaign based on response rates, conversions, and return on investment (ROI).
- Identify which segments of your audience were most responsive and why.

Optimize Your Approach

- Adjust your strategy based on the analysis to improve future campaigns.
- Consider A/B testing different elements (copy, design, offers) to find the most effective combinations.

Build Relationships

- Follow up with respondents to build and maintain relationships.
- Offer additional value through follow-ups and personalized communication.

Document Learning

- Keep detailed records of what worked and what didn't for future reference.
- Share insights with your team to improve your direct mail campaigns continuously.

Following these steps and strategies ensures that your direct mail campaign is well-planned, effectively executed, and yields the desired responses.

While our company has only done a limited mail campaign targeting foreclosures, we encourage it to help you find deals. Subscriptions to some of these services are required, and adding the mailing expenses, you must monitor what is working and what is not so your dollars are spent wisely. At HVNLY, we have found properties on Zillow.com, through real estate agents, on Auction.com, at foreclosure auctions in our local courthouse, on the HUD website, with wholesaling agents, and driving for dollars.

HVNLY Tip: "We are not what we know but what we are willing to learn."- Mary Catherine Bateson

CREATIVE FINANCING UNLOCKED

Creative financing in real estate is a guiding light for those seeking capital. But before we dive into creative financing options, let's explore the wholesaling method for those who have no money and want to get started. While our company hasn't utilized this method to create cash flow, it is trendy, especially among those starting out and those who only want to focus on finding deals and profit from finding end-buyers, the flippers who will rehab the house for a profit.

Wholesaling is a strategy where an individual, the wholesaler, enters a contract to buy a property and then sells the right to purchase it to another buyer, typically an investor, before the original contract with the seller closes. This is done by assigning the contract to the end buyer or conducting a double closing. When a contract is assigned, the wholesaler secures a property from the seller and then transfers the contract to another buyer, earning a fee based on the price difference. In a double closing, the wholesaler purchases the property and then immediately resells it to the end buyer in a second closing, profiting from the price differential between the two transactions. This method is attractive because it requires little to no capital. Yet, it still demands a deep understanding of the property market, strong negotiation skills, and the ability to find potential investors quickly. Wholesalers must also be competent and masterful at finding undervalued properties and motivated sellers.

While wholesaling can be a lucrative aspect of real estate investing, different regions have different laws that can vary significantly, so understanding these is critical. Also, remember that this strategy produces ordinary income, meaning you still need to be present and work to make money. Wholesaling might be seen as a means to an end. The end goal is to achieve financial independence with passive income.

MASTERING SELLER FINANCING: A STEP-BY-STEP GUIDE

Seller financing is a win-win for both parties. The seller acts as the lender, providing a loan to the buyer for the property purchase. This option is attractive when traditional mortgage lending criteria are a barrier for the buyer.

Understanding Seller Financing

Imagine a scenario where you're at a junction, balancing investment potential with financial constraints. Seller financing could be a great option. For sellers, it can speed up the sale, widen the buyer pool, and bring in more income through interest. At the same time, buyers may find more room to negotiate down payments and interest rates than traditional bank loans.

Negotiation Strategies

Negotiating a seller financing deal is like playing chess, where strategy, foresight, and understanding your opponent's position are essential. Start by researching the seller's motivations—are they looking for a quick sale or hoping to maximize income? With this knowledge, buyers can propose terms that meet the seller's needs while protecting their financial interests. Remember, it's all about finding a balance where both parties' goals align.

Structuring the Deal

The structure of a seller financing agreement includes the interest rate, often higher than bank rates, to offset the seller's risk. The loan term balances the buyer's ability to repay with the seller's timeline for recovering their investment. The down payment reduces the seller's risk and shows the buyer's commitment. A promissory note and a mortgage or deed of trust used to secure the agreement provide legal protection for both parties.

Success Stories and Pitfalls

There are many examples of successful seller financing deals that benefit both parties. When a property is on the market with no interest from traditional buyers and an investor sees its potential but can't secure financing conventionally, then seller financing might be the best option. With seller financing, the seller gets the sale they want, and the buyer can turn the property into a profitable venture.

However, there are risks; poorly structured agreements or not checking the other party's financial stability could derail things, which is why it's important to do your research, have a detailed agreement, and maybe seek advice from a real estate attorney.

Case Study

A few years back, a house was being sold on the SW side of our hometown. The seller lived out of town and wanted a quick sale. Unfortunately, our company could not secure conventional financing at the time since most of our income came from rentals reported on a corporate tax return. Because our income tax showed weak numbers, we couldn't qualify for any conventional loans. To do so, we needed to earn more on paper.

After some negotiation, the seller agreed to owner-financing with favorable terms for both parties. We closed the deal within 48 hours, and that three-bedroom, 2.5-bath, two-story single-family home is still part of our rental portfolio. So, in the end, the seller made the fast sale they so urgently needed, and our company acquired an asset that would produce long-lasting passive income.

Property Details:

Built in 2007 with 1,947 sq ft of living space, this asset was acquired for a promising $128,100 30-year term at 6.78% in 2017. Both parties agreed to 10% down, $12,810, and monthly payments (P & I) of $750. It has been a cash-flowing rental ever since. Additionally, we refinanced it in 2021 for a lower interest rate of 5.25% and pulled out cash to purchase another property. As this book is being written, this property has a market value of $245,000, a mortgage of $124,500, a PITI of $1,204 (P & I= $687), and a monthly rental price of $1,575.

Seller Financing Checklist

This checklist can help you understand seller financing. Use it as a guide through the negotiation and structuring of your deal to reduce risk and ensure successful investment outcomes:

- **Seller Motivation Assessment:** Understand why the seller is considering seller financing.
- **Financial Due Diligence:** Conduct thorough financial vetting of both parties.
- **Agreement Terms Negotiation:** Focus on interest rate, repayment term, and down payment.
- **Legal Documentation:** Ensure a promissory note and mortgage or deed of trust are executed correctly.
- **Exit Strategy Planning:** Have clear plans for both parties if the financing arrangement needs to be revised or canceled.

Seller financing is known for its flexibility, accessibility, and customization. With a bit of creativity and strategic planning, barriers to real estate investment can be overcome, opening new, otherwise inaccessible opportunities.

Lease Options Basics

In real estate financing, lease options offer another way to overcome traditional barriers to property ownership. A lease option combines renting with the option to buy the property later. The agreement allows the tenant to purchase the property at a set price before the lease ends.

This arrangement is an excellent option for buyers on the cusp of homeownership and sellers looking to attract buyers who may be facing financial or credit challenges. It's a chance for buyers to lock in today's prices and build equity through rent premiums or option fees credited toward the purchase. At the same time, sellers benefit from the steady rental income and the potential of a future sale under more favorable market conditions.

Finding Lease Option Opportunities

Finding properties suitable for lease option agreements requires an eye for market trends and seller circumstances. These opportunities often arise in markets with high inventory and low demand, where sellers are open to creative solutions. Properties that struggle to sell due to unique features or minor flaws are also good candidates.

Look for listings that have been on the market for a long time, talk to sellers at open houses, or work with real estate agents experienced with creative financing. The key here is understanding the property and the seller's situation. Motivated sellers, such as those relocating or dealing with inherited property, are often more willing to consider flexible selling strategies.

Negotiating the Terms

Negotiating a lease option should be done with mutual benefit in mind. It starts with the option fee, a non-refundable payment that secures the right to purchase. This fee shows the buyer's commitment and gives the seller some security.

Usually one to three years in, there will be another negotiation. This time allows buyers to improve their credit or save for a down payment. Rent premiums (extra amounts above-market rent) are also up for negotiation, helping buyers build equity in the property.

Every aspect, from the purchase price to maintenance responsibilities, should reflect a shared vision, where a successful transition means both the renter and owner end up in a stronger financial position.

Legal Considerations

The legal framework of lease options is critical for their stability and protection. A detailed lease agreement and an option contract clearly outline each party's rights and responsibilities. Having both documents ensures compliance with regulations and helps prevent disputes.

The option should specify the purchase price, option period, and terms for exercising it. Clauses regarding maintenance, property changes, and contingencies strengthen the agreement, protecting both the tenant and landlord.

It is always wise to involve an experienced real estate lawyer to draft or review these documents. This is an investment in the agreement's strength and the future it aims to secure.

"SUBJECT-TO" DEALS: HOW TO TAKE OVER PROPERTY PAYMENTS SAFELY

The Concept of Subject-To Investing

Subject-to-investing is a strategy that offers unique benefits. It involves acquiring property by taking over a seller's mortgage payments without formally assuming the loan. Here, the property's deed transfers to the buyer, but the mortgage remains in the seller's name, allowing the buyer to control and benefit from the property without securing new financing.

This approach is an example of the flexibility and creativity of real estate transactions. It offers a solution to sellers looking to escape mortgage obligations and provides buyers with a way to own property without having to jump through traditional lending hurdles. These deals are especially attractive when interest rates rise because buyers can benefit from the seller's lower interest rate on the existing mortgage.

Risk Management

However, like anything else, subject-to-investing has its challenges. For buyers, the main risk is the "due on sale" clause in the mortgage agreement, which allows the lender to demand full repayment if the property changes hands. While this clause is rarely enforced, buyers must be cautious and prepared.

On the other hand, sellers may feel uneasy about still being responsible for a mortgage they no longer control. And because their credit is tied to the loan, they rely on the buyer to make timely payments. These agreements require trust in the buyer's financial responsibility and transparency.

To reduce these risks, both parties should conduct thorough due diligence. Buyers should carefully review the property's financial status and mortgage details, and sellers should look for buyers with a solid financial track record and have a backup plan in case the buyer can't make mortgage payments.

Success Criteria

The key here is aligning the buyer's and seller's interests and expectations based on their shared confidence in the arrangement. For the buyer, success means acquiring a property potentially below market value, with immediate cash flow potential, and without the need to take out a new loan. Keeping the original loan's favorable terms can significantly increase their investment's profitability.

Sellers benefit from quick relief from mortgage obligations, often without the financial and emotional strain of foreclosure or the lengthy process of a traditional sale.

Documentation and Legalities

Documentation is crucial to protect both parties and ensure the investment's stability and legitimacy. Documents include a purchase agreement that clearly states the subject-to nature of the deal, a warranty deed transferring ownership with the mortgage remaining in the seller's name, and a buyer's acknowledgment of the existing loan terms.

Equally important is the power of attorney that the seller gives to the buyer, allowing the buyer to act on behalf of the seller regarding the mortgage. This document helps the buyer communicate with the lender, manage the loan, and address issues while maintaining transparency and integrity.

We cannot emphasize this enough that consulting with a real estate attorney experienced in subject-to-transaction deals is best. They can ensure legal compliance, make necessary disclosures to lenders, and structure the transaction to protect the rights and responsibilities of both parties.

Using Personal Networks for Investment Financing

Personal networks offer valuable financing and partnership opportunities. This can change your investment journey and benefit both parties. Leverage this resource, recognize its value, and strategically build, engage, and maintain relationships beyond just transactions.

In our business, we have developed amazing friendships with many in our network, which is one reason we are so passionate about what we do. If you are new to real estate investment, we highly recommend you join local REIA's (Real Estate Investment Associations) and support groups to start networking and learning from others.

The Power of Networking

Using personal networks in real estate investment involves more than just reaching out—it's about building connections that benefit everyone involved. Your network includes professional contacts, friends, family, and acquaintances with diverse skills, resources, and investment interests. When you engage them effectively, they can help fuel your investment projects. Start by mapping your network to find potential investors or partners whose interests match your projects. But remember, like any relationship, these need to be nurtured. Communicate regularly, share insights, and offer value without expecting immediate returns.

Pitching to Potential Investors

Balancing confidence and humility are essential when approaching potential investors in your network. Your pitch should tell a story—a compelling narrative of your vision for the property, the steps to achieve it, and the benefits for everyone involved. This story needs to be backed by a thorough analysis of the investment's potential, including risks and how you plan to mitigate them, and a clear outline of expected returns. However, the personal touch sells the pitch. Share your passion and invite them to partner with you.

Example of Borrowing Private Money for Real Estate Investment

Scenario:

- **Borrower:** John (you), a real estate investor.
- **Lender:** Jane, a private money lender.
- **Loan Amount:** $100,000
- **Interest Rate:** 12% simple interest
- **Loan Term:** 1 year.

Borrower's Perspective

John finds a promising property that he believes can be renovated and sold for a profit. He needs $100,000 to purchase and renovate the property but wants to avoid traditional bank financing due to the lengthy approval process and stringent requirements. Instead, he approaches Jane, a private money lender, who agrees to lend him the money at 12% simple interest for one year. The interest-only payments are due monthly.

Loan Details:

Principal Amount: $100,000
Annual Interest Rate: 12%
Interest Calculation:

- Simple interest means that the interest is calculated only on the principal amount, not on any accumulated interest.
- Annual Interest Payment = Principal × Interest Rate
- Annual Interest Payment = $100,000 × 12% = $12,000

Borrower's Benefits:

1. **Quick Funding:** John gets access to the funds much faster than he would through traditional bank financing, allowing him to purchase and start renovations on the property promptly.
2. **Flexibility:** Private lenders often offer more flexible terms and fewer bureaucratic hurdles than banks.
3. **Potential Profit:** John expects to sell the renovated property for $150,000. After repaying the loan principal ($100,000) and the interest ($12,000), he anticipates making a profit of $38,000 ($150,000 - $112,000).

Lender's Perspective

Jane, the lender, is looking for a high-return investment. Traditional savings accounts and CDs offer very low interest rates, typically under 2%. Jane significantly increases her returns by lending to John at 12% simple interest.

Lender's Benefits:

1. **High Return:** Jane earns $12,000 in interest on her $100,000 loan over one year, a much higher return than other low-risk investments.
2. **Fixed Income:** The simple interest loan provides a predictable income stream, with Jane knowing exactly how much she will earn by the end of the term.
3. **Collateral:** The loan is secured by the property, which means if John defaults, Jane can foreclose on the property to recoup her investment, providing an added layer of security.

Example Summary

Borrower (John):

- **Loan Amount:** $100,000
- **Interest:** $12,000 (12% of $100,000)
- **Total Repayment:** $112,000
- **Potential Sale Price of Property:** $150,000
- **Profit After Repayment:** $38,000

Lender (Jane):

- **Initial Investment:** $100,000
- **Interest Earned:** $12,000
- **Total Return:** $112,000
- **Annual Return on Investment (ROI):** 12%

By borrowing private money at 12% simple interest, John can quickly and effectively fund his real estate project, potentially making a substantial profit. Meanwhile, Jane benefits from a high return on her investment, significantly better than typical savings or low-risk options. This arrangement provides a win-win situation for both the borrower and the lender.

So do not be shy in approaching a lender when you are the John of this story. Remember that you are offering a handsome return on a collateralized loan.

If you are Jane of this story, this is an excellent way to invest in real estate without being directly involved. Lending your money time and time again will create passive income.

Structuring Partnership Deals

Creating partnership deals within your network requires trust and caution. These deals need clear roles, responsibilities, and returns to align and protect everyone's expectations. The structure can range from simple joint ventures with proportional profit sharing to more complex agreements with preferred returns for silent partners. No matter the arrangement, clear communication, and legal documentation are essential. Contracts are crucial for preserving trust and commitment, safeguarding the relationship, and ensuring the integrity of the investments.

Maintaining Relationships

Maintaining relationships thoughtfully can help keep your network strong and supportive. This means more than just occasional updates or casual conversations; it means recognizing and celebrating your contacts' achievements and milestones. Actively listening for ways to connect with people in your network helps create a supportive community, while sharing lessons learned can build trust and openness. Your network should be a community where value is exchanged through knowledge, experience, and support, not just through financial gain.

Collaboration can significantly expand the scope and effectiveness of your investments, potentially leading to exponential growth. Your network may start as a list of contacts, but it will evolve into a community of partners that accompanies you through the ups and downs of real estate investing.

CROWDFUNDING REAL ESTATE DEALS: A MODERN APPROACH

Introduction to Real Estate Crowdfunding

Crowdfunding has revolutionized access to property markets, allowing individual investors to participate in real estate projects with a fraction of the typical capital required. It is one option that allows people interested in real estate but not wanting to deal with the ins and outs of it to invest without having direct day-to-day involvement.

Real estate crowdfunding pools resources to fund projects like commercial developments or residential renovations. This approach expands the investor pool, making real estate investment more accessible and offering all investors equal opportunity.

Choosing the Right Platform

Choosing the right crowdfunding platform shapes both the course and the odds of a successful endeavor. Factors to consider include:

- The platform's track record
- The diversity and scope of its projects
- The transparency of its operations

Each platform chooses specific opportunities based on its selection criteria and fees. Thoroughly researching these factors, checking the platform's compliance with regulations, and reading user reviews will help you choose an investment that matches your risk tolerance, timeline, and financial goals.

Also, the platform's dedication to education, communication, and support systems is essential for helping investors understand and navigate crowdfunding investments while making them feel informed and supported.

Risks and Rewards

Crowdfunding in real estate is appealing because it offers both tangible rewards and opens investment opportunities to more people. Investors can earn a share of profits from property development, rehabilitation, or rental income, giving them a direct stake in real estate projects. Crowdfunding lets investors spread their investment across different properties and projects, reducing risk.

However, real estate crowdfunding has its drawbacks. Fluctuating markets, project delays, and the risk of projects not meeting expectations create uncertainties. These investments can't be easily converted to cash, as they involve long-term commitments with uncertain outcomes. Additionally, investors must rely on platform due diligence to assess projects. Managing these risks requires a cautious approach, balancing the potential rewards against the realities.

Case Studies

In our local downtown area, a run-down urban area was transformed into a mix of homes and shops thanks to hundreds of small investors. This project faced urban redevelopment complexities but reaped significant returns, revitalizing the community, and setting a model for similar ventures both in our downtown area and nationwide.

On the other hand, a luxury condo development in North Texas, promising high returns, attracted investors but faced market saturation and rising construction costs. This led to delays, tested investor patience, and highlighted the need for careful project selection and market analysis. This mishap happens more often than some would care to admit.

While different in outcomes, these stories demonstrate teamwork, innovation, and democratization of investment. They illustrate the possibilities crowdfunding offers and provide valuable insights, guiding principles, and a glimpse into collective investment potential.

NAVIGATING HARD MONEY LOANS FOR QUICK INVESTMENTS

Hard money loans offer quick access to funds for investors eyeing properties that need immediate action. These loans focus more on the property's value rather than on the borrower's credit score, making them ideal for projects conventional lenders might avoid.

Our business regularly uses hard money loans. We have used a handful of reputable lenders and have developed a business relationship with them. Partnerships are essential because terms improve once you are considered a repeat customer. While one lender might offer slightly better loan terms, another might have a speedier process. It is always good to have choices.

What Are Hard Money Loans?

Hard money loans focus more on the property's value than the borrower's financial history. They are usually offered by private investors or companies and provide short terms, lasting anywhere from six months to a few years. Interest rates can be high because the lender takes on more risk, and the loan terms are often strict and tailored to the specific project. Borrowers must negotiate carefully to ensure terms match their investment plans and abilities.

When to Use Hard Money

Hard money loans are used when quick action is required. They are ideal for distressed residential or commercial properties that need immediate attention and renovation. These loans help investors bridge the gap between acquiring and renovating the property, allowing projects to move forward quickly. Hard money loans are also helpful for investors who may not qualify for traditional financing due to credit issues or other financial challenges.

Risks and Rewards

To make use of hard money lending requires careful consideration. While these loans offer quick funding and flexible terms based on project merits, they also come with risks. Higher interest rates could eat into profits if projects face delays or market conditions change unfavorably. These short loan terms can also lead to liquidity issues if refinancing or sales don't go as planned. To control these risks, plan rigorously, craft exit strategies, and include contingencies in your investment plan.

Finding Reputable Lenders

Finding reputable lenders is important when seeking hard money loans. This involves thorough research and recommendations from experienced investors and professionals in the industry. Examining a lender's track record, reviewing past projects, and talking to previous borrowers can help determine if they are transparent, flexible, and supportive. Reviewing loan terms, fees, and how the lender handles defaults is essential to ensure they're a reliable partner. Make sure you understand the lender's practices and follow your intuition.

Hard money loans can be an excellent tool for projects requiring quick action and promising rewarding returns. However, they require careful consideration and planning. Each decision should be strategic, with a focus on achieving investment success.

USING PERSONAL LOANS AND LINES OF CREDIT WISELY

In creative real estate financing, personal loans and lines of credit are versatile tools with distinct features and uses. They offer the funding needed for investment projects but require careful management to be effective.

Personal Loans for Real Estate

Using personal loans involves using unsecured funds to finance property purchases or improvements. Unlike secured loans backed by collateral, personal loans are based on the borrower's creditworthiness, meaning interest rates can vary based on perceived risk. Yet, personal loans are attractive because they provide immediate liquidity with a fixed repayment schedule.

However, like other loan types we've discussed, personal loans come with challenges. Interest rates are often higher than secured loans, so it's crucial to calculate the investment's potential return to ensure it outweighs the financing costs. The limited repayment term also requires careful project selection and cash flow management that align with the loan's maturity.

Lines of Credit

Lines of credit are like flexible personal loans. They offer money you can use when needed, and you only pay interest on the amount you withdraw. This flexibility makes them great for real estate investors, allowing them to adjust to changing financial needs during a project. Whether you need to fill gaps in cash flow, finance renovations, or handle unexpected costs, a line of credit can keep your project moving.

However, it can be easy to borrow too much, leading to financial strain if your investments don't generate enough returns. So, managing your line of credit wisely is crucial, and only borrowing what you need can help you make sure each withdrawal adds value to your investment.

Risk Management

Navigating personal financing requires a thorough risk management strategy to protect financial well-being while investing in projects. This strategy starts with analyzing investment opportunities, predicting cash flows, and understanding how financing costs could affect profits. Sensitivity analyses can help anticipate how investments might impact market changes, interest rate fluctuations, and project delays.

Diversifying your investments helps reduce risk. By spreading your money across different projects or investments, you can lessen the impact if one doesn't perform as expected. It's also essential to have a contingency reserve—a pool of funds set aside for unexpected challenges.

Case Studies

When we first started, we purchased foreclosures at the courthouse with proceeds from the sale of another business. Paying for these foreclosures in cash, we ran out of money quickly after just a few houses. We had discovered how powerful real estate is for passive income, but we needed a way to move forward. We turned to a personal loan for the next rental property's down payment, backed by a detailed rental income analysis and market trends. We did this a few times with a local bank offering us $16,000 of unsecured funds and pulling cash from credit cards offering 0% interest. However, when you do this, it's important to have a plan in place to pay back the debt responsibly. For us, this calculated risk paid off, leading to a profitable investment and the start of a successful portfolio.

As previously mentioned, the business we bought and sold opened the doors for us to start in real estate. It was purchased in 2003 under an SBA loan requiring a 10% down payment for the purchase price of $750,000. We got creative and used a home equity line of credit for the down payment. Three years later, the business was sold for $1.25M, a healthy profit, giving us the financial means to build passive income through more real estate investments.

Diverse financing strategies offer both risk and opportunity. For savvy investors they can open doors to new possibilities and contribute to a diverse investment portfolio. Success lies in balancing risk and reward, making informed decisions, and staying committed to financial goals.

UNDERSTANDING A SELF-DIRECTED IRA AND ITS ROLE IN RE INVESTMENTS

Self-Directed Individual Retirement Accounts (SDIRAs) allow investors to grow their retirement savings by investing in assets like real estate. These flexible accounts allow investors to use their retirement funds, earn higher returns, and diversify their portfolios. SDIRAs are appealing because they offer a wide range of investment options and come with tax advantages, such as tax deferral or exemption, depending on the type of IRA.

Setting Up a Self-Directed IRA

To set up a Self-Directed IRA for real estate investing, you must choose a custodian or trustee to manage these assets. Not all custodians offer real estate options, so selecting one that does and that provides the level of service you need is crucial. A good custodian will offer a platform for real estate investments and guide the rules and regulations that apply to these transactions. It's also important to consider the fees associated with the account, as these can vary and affect your overall investment returns.

Funding Your Self-Directed IRA

You can fund your Self-Directed IRA in several ways, such as by making direct contributions, rolling over funds from other retirement accounts, or transferring money from existing IRAs or 401(k)s. Each method has its own IRS rules and limits.

Direct contributions are limited each year but provide a steady way to increase your IRA's funds. Rollovers and transfers allow you to combine retirement assets into your SDIRA, potentially giving you more capital for real estate investments. However, following the rules closely is essential to avoid unexpected taxes or penalties.

Identifying Investment Properties

Once you've set up and funded your SDIRA, the next step is to find properties that match your investment strategy and comply with IRA regulations. Look for residential, commercial properties, and even undeveloped land. But keep in mind that there are factors, such as market trends, location, and the property's unique features, that affect risk and potential return. When choosing properties, consider their potential for appreciation and income, as well as how they fit with your IRA's need for liquidity and distribution requirements.

Making the Investment

Investing in real estate through an SDIRA involves having the custodian purchase the property on behalf of the IRA, meaning the property title is held in the name of the IRA, not the individual. This ownership structure means that all financial aspects of the property, including acquisition and maintenance costs and income generated, are linked to the IRA. To maintain the IRA's tax-advantaged status, follow the IRA's rules meticulously, ensuring that all expenses and revenues flow directly through the IRA.

Managing the Investment

Managing real estate within an SDIRA involves ongoing responsibilities, including maintaining the property, handling repairs, and making improvements, all funded by the IRA to keep its tax advantages. Managing tenants for rental properties involves setting up lease agreements to collect rent. Property management must be carefully documented and executed within the IRA's guidelines. The investor must work through the custodian to ensure that all operations comply with IRS regulations to avoid prohibited transactions that could risk the IRA's tax-advantaged status.

Reaping the Benefits

Investing in real estate within an SDIRA can yield tax-advantaged growth. This means any rental income, property appreciation, or profits from sales can grow without being taxed immediately. For traditional IRAs, taxes are deferred until you start taking distributions in retirement. On the other hand, Roth IRAs offer tax-free growth, meaning you won't pay taxes on qualified distributions in retirement. This tax advantage can boost your retirement savings.

Complying with IRS Rules

To successfully manage an SDIRA with real estate investments, closely following IRS rules is crucial. Prohibited transactions, especially those involving self-dealing or benefiting disqualified persons, must be avoided to prevent the IRA from losing its tax advantages. Understanding contribution limits and distribution rules is essential for staying compliant and maximizing the IRA's tax benefits. Consult with tax advisors or legal professionals to navigate these complex regulations.

Using an SDIRA for real estate investment opens new possibilities; careful selection, diligent management, and strict adherence to regulations can enhance your portfolio and offer tax-efficient handsome returns.

THE BRRRR METHOD: A COMPREHENSIVE GUIDE FOR INVESTORS

The BRRRR method—Buy, Rehab, Rent, Refinance, Repeat—is a way to turn undervalued properties into sources of ongoing income and increasing value. We briefly cover it in this chapter, as included in creative financing. We will further dissect the BRRRR method as an expansive wealth-builder in Chapter 5.

Breaking Down BRRRR

The BRRRR method begins with buying properties below market value that often need repairs. After purchase, the property is renovated to increase its value and attract renters. Once renovated, renting out the property generates income to cover costs and provide profit. The property is then refinanced at a higher value, allowing the investor to recover most of their initial investment. The process is then repeated, using the equity and income from one property to finance the purchase of another.

Finding the Right Property

Look for properties that have the potential to increase in value after renovations, especially if they're not currently in good condition. Locate a distressed property to rehab, and you have found yourself a jewel. These properties tend to be in up-and-coming neighborhoods or have unique qualities that, when improved, can attract higher rents. Researching the market thoroughly is essential, focusing on areas with growing job opportunities, better infrastructure, and a rising population. These areas are more likely to increase property values, making refinancing and recouping your investment more manageable.

Financing the BRRRR Strategy

In the BRRRR method, investment funding involves combining acquisition and renovation financing. Initially, investors often use hard money loans, private lenders, or personal connections to finance the purchase and renovations. While more expensive than traditional mortgages, these options offer the speed and flexibility needed to acquire and improve properties quickly. Once the property is renovated and rented out, transitioning to a conventional mortgage for refinancing is extremely important. This can significantly reduce the cost of borrowing and pull out any equity created through renovations, which can be used for new investments. Successful refinancing depends on the property's increased value and ability to generate rental income, so careful renovations and efficient property management are key. Please note that in most markets, a conventional mortgage might not be an option, but refinancing with investor-friendly lenders is very doable.

Scaling Your Portfolio

To efficiently expand your real estate portfolio using the BRRRR method, you must maintain a disciplined approach to reinvestment and portfolio management. Each cycle should help you improve your criteria for property selection, renovation strategies, and financing based on experience and market trends. As the portfolio grows, you should work on establishing efficient systems for property management, tenant relationships, and financial tracking. Building solid relationships with lenders, contractors, and real estate professionals can also streamline each phase of the BRRRR process, helping you grow your portfolio faster and more sustainably.

The BRRRR method benefits individual investors and contributes to community vitality and the real estate market, showing how interconnected investment success and societal prosperity are.

Diverse financing strategies offer both risk and opportunity. For savvy investors they can open doors to new possibilities and contribute to a diverse investment portfolio. Success lies in balancing risk and reward, making informed decisions, and staying committed to financial goals.

HVNLY Tip: "The most difficult thing is the decision to act, the rest is merely tenacity." ~ Amelia Earhart ~

SETTING UP FOR INVESTING SUCCESS

A real estate investor's journey is usually filled with unexpected challenges and opportunities that can test their determination. Success in this field requires the ability to adapt to changing markets, learn from setbacks, and persevere in the face of adversity. This chapter explores the mental toughness needed to succeed, providing strategies for building resilience, turning failures into lessons, persisting through obstacles, and finding inspiration from successful investors.

BUILDING A RESILIENT INVESTOR MINDSET

Cultivating Resilience

Resilience means maintaining perspective, managing stress, and focusing on long-term goals. Techniques include:

- Setting achievable expectations.
- Breaking down big goals into smaller tasks.

- Practicing mindfulness to stay present and reduce anxiety.

Reflect on past challenges, recognize the strategies that helped you overcome them, and document these experiences. Reflection can build a mental toolkit for handling future obstacles.

Learning from Failure

Failure is a natural part of investing that offers valuable lessons for future success. It's important to see these experiences as feedback and not as a judgment of one's abilities. When a deal goes wrong, or a property doesn't perform as expected, conduct a thorough analysis to understand what went wrong and why. This involves reviewing due diligence processes, reevaluating market analysis methods, and addressing knowledge gaps. By doing this, you'll see setbacks as opportunities for learning and improving decision-making while helping you refine strategies.

The Importance of Persistence

Persistence is needed to reach long-term objectives, especially given market fluctuations. It involves sticking to the plan, even during challenging times. Persistence requires a firm belief in goals and the confidence that hard work will eventually pay off.

Setting smaller goals that align with the bigger picture can keep motivation high because accomplishing milestones brings a sense of achievement. Moreover, having a support system of mentors, colleagues, and advisors can provide encouragement and guidance, strengthening your determination to keep going.

Resilience Reflection Exercise

To strengthen your investor mindset, try this exercise:

1. *Identify a Setback:* Think about a recent challenge or failure in your investing efforts.
2. *Analyze Your Response*: Reflect on how you initially reacted to this setback. Did you see it as a defeat or a chance to learn?
3. *Extract Lessons*: Write down key lessons learned about real estate investing, decision-making, and personal growth from this experience.
4. *Plan for Future Application*: Think about how you can use these lessons in the future. What specific strategies will you adjust based on what you've learned?
5. *Share and Discuss*: If you're comfortable, talk about your reflections with a mentor or peer. Conversations can offer more insights and strengthen your support system.

This exercise can help you make a habit of learning from every experience, ensuring that each setback contributes to your growth.

Building a resilient mindset involves:

- Practicing intentionally.
- Learning from every experience.
- Drawing motivation from successful individuals who have shown persistence and adaptability.

THE ART OF NETWORKING IN REAL ESTATE CIRCLES

Success goes beyond spotting lucrative deals; it involves building a solid network. By connecting with key players, you can discover hidden opportunities, understand market trends, and build partnerships that enhance your portfolio. Networking relies on specific principles and strategies tailored to the industry, especially in real estate.

Networking Essentials

Networking is built on authenticity and mutual benefit. Unlike some industries, real estate values deep, quality connections. So, it's important that you approach networking with a focus on building long-lasting relationships rather than quick wins. This requires understanding the needs, challenges, and goals of others and providing help and support without expecting immediate returns. Work on building a foundation of trust and respect because only then will relationships bring lasting benefits.

Building Meaningful Connections

Building valuable relationships starts with strategically engaging at different levels. Reach out directly to individuals whose expertise, position, or investments align with your goals. Find common ground, exchange insights, and discuss industry trends. In addition to one-on-one connections, getting involved in shared projects, partnerships, or investment opportunities can strengthen relationships.

Leveraging Social Media

Today, social media platforms offer excellent opportunities to grow your network and establish your presence. Platforms like

LinkedIn, Facebook, and specialized real estate forums are great for sharing insights, highlighting successes, and interacting with industry leaders, potential partners, and clients.

Sharing content that shows your expertise or investment approach can attract a following and initiate conversations. Engaging in discussions, providing valuable feedback, and recognizing others' accomplishments can also boost your visibility and credibility.

Networking Events and Groups

Networking at industry events, meetups, and investment clubs is very important. To make the most of these events, be prepared to talk about your goals and challenges. Engaging in discussions, asking good questions, and following up with personalized messages can help you turn meetings into valuable connections.

Participating in investment clubs or real estate associations can help strengthen relationships, providing a platform for sharing knowledge and collaboration. By building authentic, strategic digital connections, you can navigate the complexities of the real estate market with confidence.

Today, every conversation and connection can lead to possibilities. Mastering the art of networking is a skill you can't afford to neglect.

TIME MANAGEMENT STRATEGIES FOR BUSY INVESTORS

In real estate, things move quickly, so it's important to manage your time efficiently. For investors managing portfolio growth and personal responsibilities, efficient time management can make the difference between seizing opportunities and missing out. Here, we'll discuss ways to prioritize tasks, use automation and delegation, balance work and personal life, and improve research and analysis to make better decisions.

Prioritizing Tasks

Prioritizing well entails evaluating tasks, distinguishing between those that directly impact revenue generation and those that are more administrative in nature. Reviewing your daily activities and identifying tasks that demand immediate attention versus those that can be deferred or outsourced can help you prioritize tasks better.

The Eisenhower Matrix, a tool that categorizes tasks based on urgency and importance, empowers investors to concentrate on activities that significantly advance their investment objectives. This method lets investors focus their efforts on negotiations, property assessments, and strategic planning, fueling portfolio growth and investment returns.

Automating and Delegating

Today, investors can use automation tools to handle repetitive tasks like rent collection, lease management, and market analysis. By automating these processes, you can free up time for strategic decision-making and exploring new opportunities. Delegating tasks to team members or virtual assistants can also help manage multiple projects at once. But it's important to ensure that the people you delegate these tasks to have the skills to get them done, understand your goals, and that you foster a collaborative environment.

We confess we do not shine in automating and delegating. However, it is also true that everything we do is a personal choice and a way to stay active.

Balancing Investing with Personal Life

Balancing a growing real estate portfolio with personal interests and family can be challenging and requires careful planning and setting clear boundaries between work and personal life. By sticking to a schedule, you can prevent work from spilling over into personal time, ensuring that both aspects of your life get the attention they need.

Hobbies, exercise, or spending time with loved ones can offer a much-needed break, rejuvenating your mental and emotional well-being. It can boost productivity and creativity professionally. Those who know us personally know we are passionate about travel. Fortunately, we have built a reliable and trusted team that gets the job done even while we're away. Without a doubt, this takes years and consistent dedication to develop and tune, but it is well worth it.

Efficient Research and Analysis

Making informed investment decisions requires efficient research and analysis. Use online databases, analytical tools, and subscription-based services to gather and interpret data on market trends, property values, and investment opportunities. Evaluating potential investments based on factors like location, market demand, and financial performance can help save time. You can quickly assess investments and make informed decisions by improving research techniques. This is a game changer.

LEVERAGING TECHNOLOGY FOR MARKET ANALYSIS AND MANAGEMENT

Having timely and accurate information is key to making decisions. Advanced digital tools allow you to access resources that can improve market analysis, simplify property management, and make investment tracking more precise. Make sure you take advantage of these to navigate market changes and assess property valuations using the data you collect.

Tech Tools for Investors

Real estate investors now have access to advanced technology tools to streamline and improve every aspect of the investment process. These tools include cloud-based property management systems that offer instant access to financials, tenant details, and maintenance requests, as well as analytical engines that analyze market trends and investment returns. Geographic Information Systems (GIS) technology can help visualize demographic and economic data on a map, providing detailed insights into market dynamics. Customer Relationship Management (CRM) software helps manage leads and relationships efficiently, ensuring potential deals are well-tracked. You can significantly reduce operational inefficiencies by carefully selecting and integrating these tools into your workflow.

Data-Driven Decision Making

When investing, the key is using data to make informed decisions instead of relying on gut feelings. Analyze property prices, rental rates, and market trends to pinpoint promising investment opportunities and predict changes in the market. Use tools that process real estate data using algorithms to forecast market trends to reduce risks and increase profits. Using data-driven methods to assess potential investment properties based on location, past performance, and expected profits can aid in making smart choices that match your financial goals and risk tolerance. This analytical approach, powered by technology, gives more people access to valuable information that was once only available to industry experts.

Online Resources for Continuous Learning

It is crucial to keep learning about new trends, rules, and techniques. There are loads of online platforms, classes, and resources that make it easy to keep learning. Websites like Coursera, Udemy, and specialized real estate education sites offer a range of courses, from basic property management to advanced investment analysis, taught by experts and professors. Additionally, online forums and communities let investors swap knowledge, share stories, and ask for advice, creating a culture of collaborative learning. Actively using these resources and being open to new ideas and changes ensures that the strategies you rely on are still relevant.

Staying Ahead of Market Trends

In a market that goes through ups and downs, being able to predict and react to trends can help you stay ahead. Again, technology provides tools that track real-time economic signals, rule changes, and new market trends. Services that offer detailed reports and real estate market analyses through subscriptions are also helpful. Additionally, predictive analytics use past data and machine learning to forecast market changes so you can adjust your strategies appropriately. By taking a proactive approach, you'll be able to spot opportunities early on, which will give you an edge.

LEGAL CONSIDERATIONS IN CREATIVE REAL ESTATE TRANSACTIONS

Knowing the law well is not just helpful—it is necessary. This is because property transactions are governed by a complex set of laws and rules. Every stage, from buying to selling, involves legal risks that can catch inexperienced investors off guard. You need to be proactive about following the law, have a careful plan to protect your assets and be aware of potential legal issues that could disrupt your goals.

Navigating Legal Requirements

The legal rules behind creative real estate deals go beyond basic property laws. They include a mix of different laws and regulations that can vary depending on where you are and the type of deal you're doing.

For investors using strategies like seller financing, lease options, or the BRRRR method, each strategy comes with its own legal issues. These can range from ensuring contracts are legally binding to following lending rules and tenant rights. You must truly understand and comply with these rules, paying close attention to detail and being thorough in every contract you make. It's important to keep learning and stay alert to legal changes because the rules can change, and it's your responsibility to keep up with them.

Protecting Your Investments Legally

Legally protecting your real estate investments and personal assets involves more than just having insurance. It includes setting up legal structures strategically. One common tactic is using limited liability companies (LLCs), which can help shield your personal assets from lawsuits and make property management and tax planning more efficient. However, for these structures to work, you need to follow operational rules carefully and keep your financial activities separate. It's also important to understand the legal details of these structures, such as state-specific rules and how they apply if you're investing across state lines. This protective strategy can be complicated, but it will reduce risk and ensure your success in the long run.

Common Legal Pitfalls

The real estate world is full of legal risks that can catch even experienced investors off guard. These include breaking zoning laws, violating contracts, or getting into disputes over property ownership. When using creative financing or other unique ways to buy property, you need to be extra careful to avoid breaking lending laws and rules that protect consumers. Making legal mistakes can lead to serious consequences like fines, lawsuits, losing properties, and reputational harm. To avoid these, do thorough research and actively manage potential legal issues before they become serious problems.

Seeking Legal Advice

Having an experienced real estate lawyer by your side is not just helpful—it's essential. They can navigate complex rules and foresee and prevent potential legal problems. They play a crucial role in setting up deals, writing and reviewing contracts, and making sure everything follows the law. Plus, if any legal issues do come up, they can guide you on the best way to handle them. Working closely with a lawyer early on can help you avoid many legal headaches.

Legal matters are a part of successful real estate investing, where risks and rewards go hand in hand. From understanding the many legal rules that govern property deals to setting up structures that protect your assets, expert legal advice is invaluable. Addressing legal issues with knowledge and strategy can strengthen your portfolio and help you confidently pursue creative and profitable real estate deals.

Success in this field requires more than just financial savvy or market knowledge. It comes from a combination of legal compliance, careful planning, and ongoing learning. With this solid foundation, you can achieve lasting success, overcome challenges, and seize opportunities.

HVNLY Tip: The first step toward success is taken when you refuse to be a captive of the environment in which you first find yourself. – Mark Caine

THE BRRRR METHOD - ENOUGH TO ACHIEVE FINANCIAL INDEPENDENCE

This strategy is our favorite because it has helped us achieve financial independence and grow our wealth exponentially — so we're dedicating an entire chapter to it. The BRRRR method is a comprehensive path to wealth creation, blending and cycling several key elements. This approach involves buying properties, renovating them, finding tenants, refinancing, and repeating the process. While this process has existed forever, the term BRRRR was coined by investor Brandon Turner in 2017 and was widely spread through Bigger Pockets podcasts.

The first phase of the BRRRR method, buying properties, is critical, as it lays the foundation for the entire investment process.

BUY - PICKING THE RIGHT PROPERTIES FOR BRRRR

Identifying High-Potential Properties

Homes that are great for the BRRRR method are usually priced low because of short-term issues like a rushed sale or because they need a little TLC. Sometimes, they are seriously distressed, which can be a huge advantage. Savvy investors look past these problems and imagine how the house will turn out after some updates. They know what's up in the market, what's happening in the neighborhood, and what features will draw in renters and future buyers.

Analyzing the Market

When analyzing the market for BRRRR properties, look beyond the basics. Dive into local and regional economic indicators, such as employment rates, population growth, and ongoing development projects. Areas with high rental demand typically offer great accessibility, amenities, and community quality. For example, a neighborhood with many new businesses and infrastructure projects might indicate increasing housing demand, making it a good investment opportunity. Tools like comparative market analysis (CMA) reports and real estate databases can help you find areas where property value will likely increase and offer good rental income prospects.

The Importance of Due Diligence

In the buying phase, you'll conduct thorough checks to ensure there are no unexpected issues with the property that could cause problems later. This includes inspections for structural issues, searches to ensure no liens on the property, and checks to ensure the property complies with zoning laws. This will allow you to avoid potential obstacles and confidently move forward. This step can also facilitate a favorable price negotiation process. This has been a powerful tool to renegotiate a contract price based on inspection reports in our business.

Negotiating Purchase Prices

During price negotiations, find a balance between meeting the seller's needs and ensuring the deal fits your investment goals. This involves presenting market data to justify offers, highlighting the benefits of a quick sale, and structuring terms to reduce upfront costs. The purpose here is to secure the property at a price that creates a win-win situation for both buyer and seller.

BRRRR Property Evaluation Checklist

To make choosing a property for the BRRRR method easier, follow this checklist:

1. Market Viability: Check economic indicators, rental demand, and neighborhood development.
2. Property Potential: Look for properties below market value due to cosmetic damages, seller circumstances, or temporary market conditions.
3. Rehab Scope: Estimate rehab costs to align with the after-repair value (ARV) and investment return goals.
4. Legal Compliance: Conduct title searches, zoning compliance checks, and property inspections to uncover potential issues.
5. Negotiation Strategy: Prepare market data and flexible terms to support negotiation efforts. Aim for a purchase price that accommodates rehab and holding costs.

This checklist simplifies property evaluation, laying a solid foundation for all other phases. Each move you make here, from property selection to market analysis, due diligence, and negotiation, requires foresight, planning, and a deep understanding of the playing field. You must anticipate challenges, adapt strategies, and make calculated decisions that set you up for success.

REHAB - BUDGETING AND MANAGING YOUR RENOVATIONS

The rehabilitation phase is crucial, requiring a balance between vision and practicality. This stage transforms a property into an asset and involves careful financial planning, contractor selection, project management, and strategic improvements.

Creating a Realistic Budget

Begin by creating a budget that covers all expenses while being financially sensible. This budget involves more than estimates; it should be a detailed plan for costs like materials, labor, permits, and unforeseen issues. Precision requires breaking down tasks and estimating costs using market research and quotes from suppliers and contractors. This ensures all expenses are covered and allows flexibility in adjusting to market changes or surprises during renovation.

It's important to differentiate between essential repairs that add value and superficial changes, prioritizing investments that maximize return. Our experience has been that there are almost always surprises, both small and not-so-small, along the way. So, it helps when you plan for the unexpected.

Selecting the Right Contractors

Selecting the right contractors for your rehab project is crucial. Look for professionals who offer reliability, quality work, and efficiency rather than just going with the lowest bid. Check references, review portfolios, and verify credentials to ensure they meet local regulations. It's important to find contractors who understand your vision and are committed to staying on budget and schedule. Negotiate clear terms like deliverables, timelines, and payment structures, and draft detailed contracts to protect against delays and extra costs.

After years of being in this industry and having some not-so-pleasant experiences, we now hold the general contractor license and hire the sub-contractors as needed. When one of our regulars is not available, and we need to hire someone else, we have adopted a favorite question from one of our mentors when we look for recommendations, "can you refer us to an (electrician, roofer, engineer, etc.) that you **know** and can **recommend**?" We ask people we know and whose judgment we trust. This has saved us more than a few headaches along the way. Early on, we experienced fiascos dealing with unprofessional contractors, but thankfully, it did not break us.

Managing Renovation Projects

Good project management is key when fixing up a property. You must monitor closely, ensure everyone works well together, and be ready to tackle changes.

You can handle it yourself or get a pro, but either way, you should make sure everything is going as planned, the work is well done, and you're staying on budget and schedule. Visit the site often and talk with your team to keep on top of things and be ready to make quick decisions if plans need to change.

Setting clear expectations, having strong leadership, and staying focused on improving your property is key to successful project management. The bottom line is that if someone is not doing what they said they'd do, you need to let them go and cut your losses early on before they bleed you dry.

Value-Add Renovations

Specific renovations can significantly increase a property's value, rental income, and attractiveness for refinancing. Identify these by analyzing market demands and focusing on upgrades that appeal to tenants and future buyers. Upgrading kitchens and bathrooms can substantially enhance a property's appeal and rental value. Energy-efficient upgrades and modern HVAC systems that improve comfort and align with tenants' growing preference for sustainability make properties stand out in competitive rental markets. Curb appeal improvements also make a difference, things like landscaping and exterior facades, influence first impressions, rental desirability, and appraisal valuations.

Fixing up a property is all about knowing your numbers, planning wisely, understanding the market, and doing great work. This step is key for making money now and ensuring the property will bring in rent, help you borrow money again, and grow your investment portfolio. Budget carefully, pick the right people for the job, manage the project well, and make fixes that up the property's value. With a solid grip on what the market wants and a dedication to doing things right, you can be successful.

RENT - FINDING AND MANAGING THE RIGHT TENANTS

It's a big deal in real estate investing to finally rent out your property. It's when your hard work fixing up the place starts to pay off. However, you must be smart about finding and keeping good renters to keep your investment growing. It's all about being detailed, understanding people's wants, and ensuring you and potential tenants get value from the property. By experience we say the following- a proper rental application process with a thorough background check is a must. It's best to be safe than sorry.

Setting the right rent price is extremely important. This is referred to as Fair Market Value (FMV). It should hover between being competitive enough to attract tenants and being profitable for you. Look at the rental rates in your area, but also consider the unique appeal your property might have due to its location, features, or nearby services. The aim is to set a rent that not only attracts people but also guarantees a steady flow of income.

When marketing your rental, be savvy—think digital. Use online platforms, social media, and maybe even virtual tours. Make your ads pop with great photos and descriptions highlighting the best parts of living there. Get ads on popular sites and within your local community to connect with the right tenants.

When choosing the right tenants, scrutinize their rental history, credit score, job stability, and references. By being transparent and fair in your selection process, you're more likely to find tenants who will take good care of your property and respect the lease agreement.

Good tenant relationships mean being there for them, setting clear rules, and handling issues quickly and fairly. Frequent check-ins and a helpful approach to problems can go a long way. Simply put, it ensures a low turnover.

Nailing the renting process is what turns a property into a winner. Every move adds to the property's value as both a financial asset and an excellent place for tenants to call home. This method is all about building something worthwhile for everyone involved.

REFINANCE - NAVIGATING THE PROCESS AND MAXIMIZING RETURNS

The refinancing stage is the culmination of strategic buying, renovation, and renting efforts, offering the opportunity to convert equity into liquid capital for further investments. This phase requires a deep understanding of the refinancing process, property valuation, negotiation, and equity management. Each step is critical, aiming to recover invested capital, strengthen your position, and sustain the growth cycle.

Understanding Refinancing Options

Refinancing in the BRRRR method means looking at different choices, remembering that each comes with pros and cons. A traditional mortgage might give you low interest and an extended repayment time, but the bank will still look closely at how much money the property could make and your financial history. If you have several properties, a portfolio loan can simplify things with one payment, but the interest might be slightly higher. It is important to note that a portfolio loan can set limitations on being able to sell a single property within this loan simply because it is bundled up with other properties. Cash-out refinancing can give you access to more of the property's value, but you must be careful about how this procedure changes your debt compared to its valuation and how it affects its interest rate.

To make the best choice, consider your long-term money goals and what risks you're okay with. The right refinancing plan will help you keep growing your investments. Remember, when interest rates are high, like now, the BRRRR method can be more challenging. Many investors often switch strategies until the numbers make more sense.

Preparing for the Appraisal

The appraisal in the refinancing process heavily influences the loan amount and terms, so preparing for it is key. Preparation goes beyond superficial improvements and requires a strategy to showcase the property's value to the appraiser. You'll need to create a detailed portfolio of all renovations and upgrades, supported by before-and-after photos, invoices, and permits to show the enhancements made to the property. Additionally, analyzing recent sales and listings in the area can provide context, helping to determine the property's value in today's market.

The goal is to present the appraiser with a compelling story of the property's transformation, along with market trends, maximizing the assessed value and the potential for refinancing. We recently learned about how much preparation the appraisal process takes. We used to let appraisers work their own numbers, not knowing that we could heavily influence the process by providing supporting documents.

Securing the Best Refinancing Terms

Securing good refinancing terms means being persuasive and well-prepared. You must do market research and show off your property's ability to bring in cash. Look at what different lenders are offering and think about their rates, fees, repayment schedules, and any early payment costs. Having honest chats with lenders about how your property is performing, backed up by solid numbers, can give you an edge.

Stress how dependable and profitable your investment is. If you've been successful in the past and have managed properties well, that'll help you stand out. Be strategic in your conversations to shape loan terms that match your property's worth and income.

Leveraging Equity

Using the cash you get from refinancing to fund new investments is a big part of the BRRRR method's power to grow wealth. But you must do it wisely, with a well-thought-out plan that looks at the market, sets clear investment goals, and considers the risks. When you decide how to use that money, whether it's trying out different kinds of real estate or just growing your financial cushion —you need to look at the big picture and where you want to go.

The best approach is to balance borrowing to expand and maintain a manageable debt level. Each reinvestment should contribute to the growth of your portfolio and align with your financial plan. Using your refinanced cash wisely means seizing opportunities while ensuring a foundation for long-term wealth.

REPEAT - SCALING YOUR PORTFOLIO RESPONSIBLY

Growing your real estate investments with the BRRRR method is like sailing a ship without a map. Every move you make steers your financial journey. It's exciting, sure, but it takes a careful and detailed plan to keep your investments in good shape and growing.

Assessing Financial Health

Checking your financial health is vital before you decide to grow your real estate portfolio. Examine how your current investments are doing by looking at cash flow, how much profit you're making, and what your returns are for each property. This will show you what's working well and where you might be at risk.

You also need to know how much cash you have and how much you owe to ensure you can take on new properties without stretching yourself too thin. A complete financial check-up is the best way to decide and grow your portfolio.

Strategic Portfolio Expansion

When you're choosing new investments, mix things up while maintaining a balance. This approach can reduce your risk and increase your odds of reliable returns. Diversification involves:

- Exploring different types of properties and markets.
- Considering the timing of acquisitions.
- Evaluating the impact of potential economic shifts.

It is recommended to spread your investments across different real estate types – like houses, offices, and factories to have a safety net. Each type reacts to the economy in its own way, so if one goes through a rough patch, it won't drag everything else down with it. When you're looking for new properties to invest in, go for ones that add something new to what you already have or stick to what you know works well for you and your wallet. Being careful can lead to long-lasting success and help you handle the twists and turns of the real estate world.

While our company has yet to venture into different real estate types, we have chosen to invest in various residential assets, from single-family homes to duplexes and triplexes. Our diversification includes long-term, mid-term, and short-term rentals, furnished and unfurnished, and even room rentals with all utilities included.

Leveraging Lessons Learned

Looking back at your BRRRR experiences can help you understand future investments. Think about what went well and what didn't. Did specific updates make more money than you thought they would? Did some areas favor your properties more than others? Reviewing the hits and misses helps you pick properties better, plan for fixes, deal with tenants, and get loans.

Sustaining Cash Flow

Keeping your cash flow in the green is critical as your property list gets longer. It's about making sure you make money by keeping your properties occupied and costs down. Regularly check your rent prices to ensure they're right—not too low or too high, and keep a close eye on spending, whether for upkeep or mortgage payments. When you're in the middle of the BRRRR process, stick to your budget and get the renovations done on time to start renting out quickly and avoid losing money by having empty properties sit there.

Expanding your portfolio involves:

- Monitoring your financial health.
- Diversifying your investments.
- Drawing lessons from past experiences.
- Maintaining a robust cash flow.

It requires diligence, adaptability, and a commitment to continuous improvement so that each BRRRR cycle enhances the value and profitability of your investments.

Being careful helps your investments survive ups and downs and enables you to be ready to make the most of the chances that come your way. As you go on, apply these strategies to whatever new twists the real estate market throws your way.

Triplex BRRRR Case Study

Our journey with this property began with a daunting challenge-its deplorable condition. Listed at $199K, we saw potential and negotiated a deal, closing on it in September 2021 for $185K. To fund this acquisition, we went with a hard money loan, also known as a bridge loan (term loan varying from 6 to 24 months). Our 12-month bridge loan meant we needed to have a well-planned exit strategy, be it a sale or a refinance.

The triplex sits on a corner lot and consists of a 1917 building with a 2/1 (two-bedroom, one bathroom) upstairs and a 2/1 downstairs. The third unit, built in 1922, stands alone as a 3/2. Each building faces a street on this corner lot. Initially, we calculated the rehab at $90K, but unforeseen situations elevated rehab costs to $125K.

Every real estate asset has its own story, and this was no different. The downstairs tenant had lived there for 20 years and did not want to leave. Her monthly rent had been $450 for years, given the condition of the building. With holes in the floors of a pier & beam foundation and walls falling apart, rats had taken over. We agreed to fix the vacated upstairs unit first while she lived downstairs and figured out what to do next. This situation was not ideal for us, but humanizing the transaction was the right thing to do.

The transformation was remarkable. After a miraculous remodel, the upstairs unit attracted the downstairs tenant, who was willing to pay $1300 a month to rent it out. The downstairs rehab was completed shortly after and rented for $1350. Despite the challenges, the third unit, once a rehab nightmare, turned out to be a testament to the potential of the BRRRR strategy, renting for $1600.

We started the refinance process as soon as all tenants were in place. The appraisal came back at $490K, and we did a 70% LTV (loan to value) with a loan of $343K. Interest rates rose rapidly, and we secured a 30-year loan at 7.2%. Our new monthly mortgage was $2932, including taxes and insurance. With the $343K loan, we paid off the bridge loan at closing, the rehab, plus the holding costs for the duration of the rehab.

Holding costs include closing costs, monthly interest payments, utilities, insurance, and other expenses associated with the process.

BRRRR case study recap:

- Purchase Price: $185K
- Rehab: $125K
- Holding Cost: $30K
- Total Cost: $340K
- New mortgage: $343K
- Mortgage (PITI) + Reserves: $3232/month
- Rents: $4250/month
- Passive Income: $1000+/month
- Increased Net Worth: $147K

To read the entire case study posted on our business FB page on January 4, 2023, visit https://www.facebook.com/HVNLYProperty Group.

HVNLY Tip: "The desire of gold is not for gold. It is for the means of freedom and benefit. -Ralph Waldo Emerson

FLIPPING FOR PROFIT: A CLOSER LOOK

Flipping involves more than just the excitement of renovation; it requires careful planning, research, and execution. To flip houses, you must be able to see potential and value where others see problems and manage renovations and sales effectively to make a profit.

Success here relies on being able to evaluate, analyze, and take decisive action. This section discusses the crucial first step in the flipping process: assessing properties to determine their profit potential. We regularly shift between the BRRRR method and flipping based on the property being considered.

We must dissect the numbers to explain why and when we shift between choosing to keep a property in our rental portfolio or flip it. Larger properties are usually best to flip. The reason is that while they may sell at an appealing high price once remodeled, the rental numbers do not work as well. We will give a case study with applicable numbers in our area. Your market might differ. While these numbers might be lower in the real world, we have chosen 30% for operating expenses on both properties to keep congruence.

CASE STUDY 1: DIFFERENT PROPERTIES - SAME INTEREST RATE

Option 1: Cookie Cutter 3-Bedroom Home

Details:

- **Purchase Price:** $150,000
- **Renovation Costs:** $20,000
- **Total Investment:** $170,000
- **Mortgage Amount:** $150,000
- **Expected Monthly Rent:** $1,700
- **Occupancy Rate:** 95% (11.4 months/year)
- **Interest Rate:** 7%
- **Loan Term:** 30 years.

Mortgage Calculation for the 3-Bedroom Home:

1. **Monthly Mortgage Payment** (P&I only): $997.95
2. **Annual Mortgage Payment:**

- $997.95 × 12 = $11,975.40

Financials for the 3-Bedroom Home:

1. Annual Rental Income:

- $1,700/month × 11.4 months = $19,380/year

2. Operating Expenses (30% of rental income):

- $19,380 × 0.30 = $5,814/year

3. Net Operating Income (NOI):

- $19,380 - $5,814 = $13,566/year

4. Cash Flow:

- Annual Rental Income - Operating Expenses - Annual Mortgage Payment
- $19,380 - $5,814 - $11,975.40 = $1,590.60/year

Option 2: Larger, Pricier Home

Details:

- **Purchase Price:** $300,000
- **Renovation Costs:** $40,000
- **Total Investment:** $340,000
- **Mortgage Amount:** $300,000
- **Expected Monthly Rent:** $2,750
- **Occupancy Rate:** 85% (10.2 months/year)
- **Interest Rate:** 7%
- **Loan Term:** 30 years.

Mortgage Calculation for the Larger Home:

1. **Monthly Mortgage Payment** (P&I only): $1,995.90
2. **Annual Mortgage Payment:**

- $1,995.90 × 12 = $23,950.80

Financials for the Larger Home:

1. Annual Rental Income:

- $2,750/month × 10.2 months = $28,050/year

2. Operating Expenses (30% of rental income):

- $28,050 × 0.30 = $8,415/year

3. Net Operating Income (NOI):

- $28,050 - $8,415 = $19,635/year

4. Cash Flow:

- Annual Rental Income - Operating Expenses - Annual Mortgage Payment
- $28,050 - $8,415 - $23,950.80 = -$4,315.80/year (negative cash flow)

Comparison Summary

Cookie Cutter 3-Bedroom Home:

- Total Investment: $170,000
- Annual Rental Income: $19,380
- Net Operating Income (NOI): $13,566
- Annual Mortgage Payment: $11,975.40
- Cash Flow: $1,590.60/year.

Larger, Pricier Home:

- Total Investment: $340,000
- Annual Rental Income: $28,050
- Net Operating Income (NOI): $19,635
- Annual Mortgage Payment: $23,950.80
- Cash Flow: -$4,315.80/year (negative cash flow)

The cookie cutter 3-bedroom home provides a positive cash flow of $1,590.60 per year after all expenses and mortgage payments, making it a more financially sound investment. In contrast, the larger, pricier home results in a negative cash flow of $4,315.80 per year, indicating that it is not as viable for rental income under these financing conditions. This highlights the importance of considering all costs and income potentials when choosing investment properties and what strategies to use.

CASE STUDY 2: SAME PROPERTY - DIFFERENT INTEREST RATES

Property Details:

- **Purchase Price:** $150,000
- **Rehabilitation Costs:** $20,000
- **Total Investment:** $170,000
- **Expected Monthly Rent:** $1,700
- **Loan Amount:** $161,000 (purchase price + rehab costs - down payment of $9,000)
- **Loan Term:** 30 years.

Scenario 1: Mortgage at 4.5% Interest Rate

Loan Details:

- Interest Rate: 4.5%
- Loan Term: 30 years.

Mortgage Calculation:

1. Monthly Mortgage Payment (P&I only): $814.73
2. Annual Mortgage Payment:

- $814.73 × 12 = $9,776.76

Financials:

1. Annual Rental Income:

- $1,700/month × 12 months = $20,400/year

2. **Operating Expenses** (30% of rental income):

- $20,400 × 0.30 = $6,120/year

3. **Net Operating Income (NOI):**

- $20,400 - $6,120 = $14,280/year

4. **Cash Flow:**

- Annual Rental Income - Operating Expenses - Annual Mortgage Payment
- $20,400 - $6,120 - $9,776.76 = $4,503.24/year

Scenario 2: Mortgage at 8% Interest Rate

Loan Details:

- **Interest Rate:** 8%
- **Loan Term:** 30 years.

Mortgage Calculation:

1. **Monthly Mortgage Payment** (P&I only): $1,182.68
2. **Annual Mortgage Payment:**

- $1,182.68 × 12 = $14,192.16

Financials:

1. Annual Rental Income:

- $1,700/month × 12 months = $20,400/year

2. Operating Expenses (30% of rental income):

- $20,400 × 0.30 = $6,120/year

3. Net Operating Income (NOI):

- $20,400 - $6,120 = $14,280/year

4. Cash Flow:

- Annual Rental Income - Operating Expenses - Annual Mortgage Payment
- $20,400 - $6,120 - $14,192.16 = $87.84/year

Comparison summary

Mortgage at 4.5% Interest Rate:

- **Monthly Mortgage Payment: $814.73**
- **Annual Mortgage Payment: $9,776.76**
- **Annual Rental Income: $20,400**
- **Operating Expenses: $6,120**
- **Net Operating Income (NOI): $14,280**
- **Cash Flow: $4,503.24/year.**

Mortgage at 8% Interest Rate:

- **Monthly Mortgage Payment: $1,182.68**
- **Annual Mortgage Payment: $14,192.16**
- **Annual Rental Income: $20,400**
- **Operating Expenses: $6,120**
- **Net Operating Income (NOI): $14,280**
- **Cash Flow: $87.84/year.**

The mortgage interest rate significantly impacts the property's cash flow. With a 4.5% interest rate, the property generates a healthy positive cash flow of $4,503.24 annually. However, with an 8% interest rate, the cash flow drops dramatically to only $87.84 per year, barely covering expenses and leaving little margin for unforeseen costs or profits.

During these times of higher interest rates, it has made more financial sense for us to do flips rather than hold them in our rental portfolio.

ASSESSING PROPERTIES FOR FLIPPING: A COMPREHENSIVE GUIDE

Property Evaluation Criteria

Finding a property with great potential for flipping involves looking beyond just appearances. Important factors to consider when trying to maximize profitability include location, the property's current condition, market demand, and the potential for adding value.

For example, a property in a desirable neighborhood that needs significant renovations offers a balance of investment and potential profit. On the other hand, a home that needs minimal work in a slow market may yield less profit, even though it may seem ready to sell.

Market Analysis for Flippers

It is important to examine market trends in the area. This means examining recent home sale prices, how quickly homes are selling, and the types of buyers in the market. Tools like comparative market analysis (CMA) can show how similar homes nearby were priced and how long they took to sell.

For example, a property near a school or in a neighborhood with planned improvements may sell quickly and at a higher price because it appeals more to families.

Inspection and Due Diligence

A comprehensive inspection is essential for a successful flip. This will reveal any underlying issues, such as structural defects, outdated electrical wiring, or plumbing issues, that could substantially increase renovation expenses. Thorough due diligence also involves confirming the property's legal status and checking for any liens, outstanding permits, or zoning concerns that could hinder renovation efforts or future sales.

INSPECTION & DUE DILIGENCE CHECKLIST

Property Inspection

Exterior Inspection:

- **Roof:** Check for missing or damaged shingles, leaks, and overall condition.
- **Foundation:** Look for cracks, settling, or water damage.

- **Siding and Paint:** Inspect for peeling paint, cracks, and signs of moisture damage.
- **Windows and Doors:** Ensure they are in good condition, properly sealed, and functional.
- **Gutters and Downspouts:** Check for clogs, leaks, and ensure proper drainage away from the foundation.
- **Landscaping:** Evaluate the condition of lawns, trees, and plants and check for proper grading to prevent water from pooling near the foundation.
- **Driveway and Walkways:** Look for cracks, potholes, and tripping hazards.

Interior Inspection:

- **Walls and Ceilings:** Check for cracks, water stains, and signs of mold.
- **Floors:** Inspect for unevenness, stains, and damage to carpets, tiles, or hardwood.
- **Plumbing:** Test faucets, showers, and toilets; check for leaks, water pressure, and drainage.
- **Electrical Systems:** Test outlets, switches, and light fixtures; check the condition of the electrical panel and wiring.
- **Heating, Ventilation, and Air Conditioning (HVAC):** Test the furnace, air conditioner, and ventilation; check for maintenance records.
- **Appliances:** Test all included appliances (stove, refrigerator, dishwasher, etc.) for functionality.
- **Attic and Basement:** Look for signs of pests, water damage, proper insulation, and ventilation.

Structural Inspection:

- **Foundation:** Check for cracks, moisture, and structural integrity.
- **Load-Bearing Walls:** Ensure there are no unauthorized modifications that compromise structural integrity.
- **Beams and Columns:** Inspect for rot, termites, and structural soundness.

Due Diligence Checklist

Financial Analysis:

- **Purchase Price:** Verify the agreed-upon purchase price.
- **Market Analysis:** Compare similar properties (comps) in the area for value assessment.
- **Income and Expenses:** Review rent rolls, operating expenses, and maintenance costs.
- **Property Taxes:** Confirm the current property tax rate and any upcoming assessments.
- **Insurance:** Get quotes for property insurance and ensure adequate coverage.

Legal and Title Review:

- **Title Search:** Conduct a title search to check for liens, easements, and encumbrances.
- **Zoning:** Verify zoning regulations and ensure the property complies with local zoning laws.
- **Permits:** Ensure all renovations and improvements have the necessary permits.

- **HOA Rules:** Review homeowners association rules, fees, and regulations (if applicable).

Environmental Review:

- **Hazardous Materials:** Check for the presence of asbestos, lead paint, and radon.
- **Flood Zone:** Determine if the property is in a flood zone and requires flood insurance.
- **Soil Stability:** Assess soil conditions, especially in areas prone to erosion or landslides.

Tenant and Lease Review (for rental properties):

- **Current Leases:** Review existing lease agreements and tenant payment history.
- **Security Deposits:** Confirm the amount of security deposits held and their compliance with local laws.
- **Eviction History:** Check for any recent evictions or problem tenants.

Property Management:

- **Management Company:** Evaluate the experience and reputation of any current property management company.
- **Maintenance Records:** Review records of past maintenance and repairs.
- **Capital Expenditures:** Identify any major capital expenditures that may be needed in the near future.

Final Walkthrough:

- Conduct a final walkthrough before closing to ensure the property is in the agreed-upon condition.

CALCULATING ARV (AFTER REPAIR VALUE)

The After Repair Value (ARV) is the property's projected value after all renovations are completed. Calculating the ARV accurately is vital for determining the potential profit margin. This calculation involves analyzing comparable sales in the area, adjusting for differences in property features, and adding the value of planned improvements. Precision here guides the budgeting for purchase and renovation costs.

For example, if comparable properties in the neighborhood sell for significantly higher prices due to features like modern kitchens or landscaped yards, investing in similar upgrades can increase the property's ARV and profitability.

Property Evaluation Checklist for Flippers

Before committing to a flip, run through this checklist:

- **Location:** Is the property in a high-demand area? Consider proximity to amenities, schools, and future community developments.
- **Condition:** Assess the extent of repairs and renovations needed. Distinguish between cosmetic updates and significant structural work.
- **Market Analysis:** Perform a comparative market analysis (CMA) to understand local pricing trends and buyer preferences.

- **Inspection and Due Diligence:** Complete a professional property inspection. Verify legal standings, such as liens or zoning restrictions.
- **ARV Calculation:** Estimate the After Repair Value based on comparable sales and the impact of planned renovations.

This checklist provides a guide to evaluating a property's flipping potential, ensuring that decisions are informed, strategic, and aligned with profitability objectives.

The first assessment of a property guides renovation plans, budgets, and the eventual sale price. Each task, including assessing potential, market analysis, inspections, and calculating After Repair Value (ARV), demands careful attention and foresight. This phase will help you decide whether the project is viable and profitable.

FINANCING YOUR FLIP: CREATIVE SOLUTIONS TO FUNDING CHALLENGES

Obtaining the money to turn ideas into tangible assets requires exploring creative financing options. There is a range of funding choices, each with its pros and cons to consider. The key is to use these resources effectively to make the most of each investment, ensuring that the initial capital helps achieve profitability. We are revisiting the Chapter 3 matter.

Creative Financing Options

When planning a flip, you should explore flexible and accessible financing methods. One option is seller financing, where the seller funds the purchase. This speeds up closing and offers less restrictive financial checks.

Another option is assuming existing mortgages, involving taking over the seller's mortgage under its original terms.

No matter the strategy, you should have a grasp of contractual responsibilities and strong negotiation skills to secure terms that match your financial plan.

Using OPM (Other People's Money)

Using other people's money (OPM), some call it opium, involves tapping into various sources, such as private investors, investment groups, and personal contacts. This option requires presenting a convincing proposition that details the project's potential returns, timelines, and risk management strategies. Clear agreements outlining terms like interest rates, repayment schedules, and equity shares will help you align interests and inspire trust. This partnership between investors and funders allows the project to move forward with the necessary capital in the hopes of appealing returns.

Hard Money Loans and Lines of Credit

House flippers, including our company, often turn to hard money loans. We opt for these because they are short-term loans based on a property's potential rather than a borrower's credit history.

Hard money loans prioritize the property's worth and the flipper's fix-up plan, offering quick cash access. However, they tend to carry higher interest rates and demand rapid repayment. Alternatively, credit lines are more fluid, providing money as needed, which can help manage finances smoothly throughout the renovation process. These options offer speed and flexibility but come with higher costs, highlighting the need for budgeting smartly and scheduling projects carefully.

Partnerships in Flipping

Partnerships offer a way to reduce financial risk and leverage combined expertise. When formed between investors with complementary skills or resources, these partnerships enable the pooling of capital, sharing responsibilities, and diversifying investment portfolios.

Establishing partnerships involves defining roles, contributions, and profit-sharing arrangements, often formalized in a joint venture agreement. Collaborating not only spreads financial risk but also increases the project's chances of success. The idea here is that teamwork often yields better results than individual efforts.

At HVNLY Property Group, we have been involved in flipping partnerships with the sole purpose of helping others get their feet wet. We have partnered with general contractors who decided to buy a property they'd worked on, and we've partnered with a realtor who wanted to get started in flipping but was too afraid of taking the first step.

When we transform properties into profitable assets, the financing strategies we use are as different as the projects themselves. These range from innovative financing options to utilizing other people's money, hard money loans, and collaborative partnerships. Each strategy requires a customized approach based on thorough analysis and strategic planning.

THE FLIP EXECUTION: TIMELINES, CONTRACTORS, AND SALES STRATEGIES

The execution phase of a flip is when the detailed planning turns into real action, bringing your ideas to life. This stage is about imagining what could be and using a structured approach to make those ideas a reality. It includes vital steps like managing time well, working closely with contractors, using effective sales strategies, and showcasing the property effectively.

Creating a Timeline

Creating an effective timeline involves understanding the complexities of property renovation. This timeline is more than a schedule—it's a roadmap that guides the entire project. It considers both the specific tasks needed for renovation and the market conditions influencing the best time to list the property.

It's crucial to break down the renovation into distinct stages. Assign each stage a specific duration and allow extra time for unexpected issues. This will serve as your blueprint, ensuring smooth transitions, minimizing downtime, and optimizing the use of resources.

For example, planning exterior work during favorable weather reduces the risk of delays. Similarly, coordinating interior renovations with slower market periods ensures the property is ready to sell when buyer interest peaks.

Managing Contractors

Managing contractors is crucial for staying on track and on time while ensuring top-notch work at the best price. You should focus on fostering teamwork by establishing honest, responsible, and respectful relationships. Set clear expectations, monitor progress regularly, and offer incentives for meeting deadlines. It's also important to have a backup plan if a contractor is unavailable or fails to meet expectations. Hiring experienced contractors with a solid reputation, whether through recommendations or reviewing their previous work, can help minimize issues.

Effective Sales Strategies

The sale of the property marks the climax of the flipping process, where strategic planning can significantly enhance profits. Developing effective sales strategies requires being on top of market trends, understanding buyer behavior, and excellent negotiation skills. This can help you set the right price and shape marketing efforts to attract a larger pool of buyers, focusing on buyers drawn to the property's unique features.

Using digital platforms can extend your reach, but targeting strategies like hosting real estate events or leveraging professional networks can attract buyers with specific interests. Timing the market is crucial, as well as selling during favorable seasons or market conditions to improve financial outcomes.

Staging and Presentation

The final step in getting a flipped property ready for sale is staging. This is a strategic process to present the home in a way that attracts potential buyers. It's more than just decorating; it's about highlighting the property's strengths while downplaying weaknesses.

Professional staging can transform an empty house into a home, helping buyers envision its possibilities. The choice of furniture, colors, and decor is carefully picked to appeal to the target audience, and quality photos of the staged property are taken. This can improve online listings, draw more viewers, and boost the chances of a quick and profitable sale. While staging is not always necessary, and we do not regularly do it, it can be beneficial.

Avoiding Common Mistakes in Flipping Projects

One wrong move can mess up your profits and timeline. To succeed, you need to know the common pitfalls and avoid them using what you learned from experience. Move carefully, follow the plan, and deal well with problems.

Budget Overruns

Keeping a tight grip on the budget is a big deal. If you spend more than planned, your profit could take a severe hit. It's important you start with a detailed budget, not just ballpark figures.

This is not just a list of expenses but a comprehensive financial roadmap. It should leave no expense unaccounted for, from the obvious ones like materials and labor to the often-overlooked ones like permits and temporary utilities. By carefully examining each budget component, you'll better understand the project's financial needs, equipping you to make informed decisions and control spending.

To prevent budget overruns, include a financial safety net in your plan—a contingency fund. This reserve, typically 10% to 15% of your total project costs, is there for unforeseen circumstances or expenses that were not part of your initial calculations. This cushion can also absorb unexpected costs without compromising the financial stability of your project.

Planning your budget to include this extra safety cash helps protect you from overspending. It also means you can handle surprises with less stress and avoid cutting corners or ditching the project because the money's run out.

Underestimating Timelines

Time management is key in the house-flipping business. Not planning enough time for the renovation can lead to increased costs, such as having to hold onto the property longer and missing the right time to sell. Make sure you account for the time renovations may take, as delays can arise due to material shortages, a lack of available workers, or surprise repairs.

Incorporating a buffer in your timeline gives you more flexibility to handle unexpected setbacks. Keeping a close eye on your progress also lets you spot issues so that you can quickly make the necessary tweaks to stay on course.

Overcapitalizing on Renovations

When aiming to transform a property, the risk of overcapitalization—spending more on the property than it's worth in the market—can be challenging. The key to avoiding this pitfall lies in understanding what the target market wants and values. Renovations should be focused on enhancing the property in ways that appeal to potential buyers rather than going overboard with unnecessary upgrades. We have sometimes been guilty of this but justify it because we want buyers to be completely excited and in love with the property.

Invest in improvements that boost the property's value and appeal to buyers. For instance, in markets where buyers place more importance on interior finishes, it might make more sense to invest in updating the kitchen rather than splurging on landscaping.

By investing in renovation planning, focusing on elements that enhance the property's market appeal and value, you can ensure that every dollar spent contributes to a successful sale. This approach helps avoid sinking money into upgrades that don't provide a significant return on investment.

Market Fluctuations

The real estate market is constantly changing, influenced by factors like the economy, interest rates, and buyers' feelings. To navigate these ups and downs, you need to analyze the market and be flexible. Keeping an eye on market trends and economic forecasts can help you understand how property values and buyer interest shift, helping you make better decisions on when to sell.

Analysis is just as important as flexibility. You should always be open to adjusting plans based on market changes. This means speeding up renovation phases to take advantage of increased buyer interest or holding off on selling until market conditions improve. By combining market analysis with the ability to adapt, you can make the most of financial opportunities.

Each project is a mix of risk, opportunity, and strategy, so being aware and ready for potential challenges is key. By sticking to the plan and staying flexible, you can turn obstacles into manageable factors.

MARKETING YOUR FLIPPED PROPERTY FOR MAXIMUM PROFIT

We want to emphasize the importance of strategic marketing when selling a newly renovated property. This final stage of a flip is crucial for maximizing profits and ensuring a successful sale. Here are some key points to consider when positioning your renovated property in the marketplace:

1. Understand Your Target Market: Conduct market research to understand the demographics, preferences, and buying behaviors of potential buyers in the area where your property is located. This will help you tailor your marketing strategy so that you appeal to the right audience.

2. Create a Compelling Marketing Narrative: Highlight your property's unique selling points and features through compelling storytelling. Showcase before-and-after photos, emphasize the improvements made, and highlight the lifestyle benefits of living in the home.

3. Professional Photography and Staging: High-quality photos and professional staging can enhance the appeal of your property. Consider hiring a professional photographer and stager to showcase your property in the best light.

4. Online Marketing: Utilize online platforms such as real estate websites, social media, and targeted digital advertising to reach more potential buyers. Consider creating virtual tours or video walkthroughs to give buyers a better view of the property.

5. Open Houses and Private Showings: Hosting open houses and private showings can generate interest and create a sense of urgency among potential buyers. Ensure that the property is well-presented and that you or your agent are available to answer any questions.

6. Effective Negotiation: Be prepared to negotiate with potential buyers, understand the market dynamics, be flexible when necessary, and work with a skilled real estate agent if needed.

Having a strategic and refined marketing plan can increase your chances of attracting the right buyers, maximizing your profits, and achieving a successful sale.

Targeting the Right Market

To ensure a successful sale, it's essential to target the right demographic. You can create a buyer persona by considering community demographics, local amenities, and unique property features. For instance, a home near good schools may appeal to young families, while a modern downtown loft might attract professionals. Understanding these details helps tailor a marketing message that connects with potential buyers.

Digital Marketing Strategies

Using online platforms can boost visibility and help reach a wider audience with targeted marketing. A comprehensive digital marketing strategy includes professional photos, virtual tours, and social media promotion on platforms like Facebook and Instagram. By optimizing listings for search engines like Google, you can also ensure that your property shows up when buyers search online. Engaging content can create interest and emotional connections, leading to more inquiries.

Open House and Viewing Tips

Creating a memorable open house or viewing experience requires planning and attention to detail. To prepare for these events, make sure the property is clean, all minor repairs are done, and the decor is neutral to appeal to more buyers. Consider playing soft background music, using strategic lighting to highlight the space, and baking cookies to create a cozy atmosphere that helps visitors imagine themselves living there. Personal interactions are also important; be friendly, knowledgeable about the property and area, and ready to answer questions to build trust and confidence with potential buyers.

Negotiating Sales

Negotiating effectively is the best way to make a profit from a property flip. Having a good grasp of the market, being patient, and making strategic decisions are all necessary. Being able to understand the property's value based on market research and feedback from viewings gives you the confidence to stand firm on your price while being willing to consider reasonable offers. Consider setting a slightly higher asking price to allow room for negotiation or offering minor concessions, such as repairs or help with closing costs during negotiations.

Highlighting the property's best features and recent upgrades can help you secure a good deal. Balancing assertiveness with flexibility during negotiations can lead to a win-win for both parties without compromising on profits.

The process of marketing and negotiating in flipping is a semi-challenging journey that involves understanding your target market, using digital platforms to boost visibility, creating memorable viewing experiences, and mastering negotiation skills. Each step brings you one step closer to maximizing your return on investment.

The Good, The Bad & the Ugly of Flipping

Most people tend to share their success stories, profits, and the joy they get in transforming a distressed property into something beautiful. Fortunately, this is the reality of real estate investing. However, it's important to talk about those flipping deals that maybe didn't go so well, or that turned out differently than expected.

We have done several flips that barely made a profit. When a company holds a property for three to five months, holds the liability through the rehab process, and the sale yields only a $5K profit, this is perceived as a total and absolute failure.

Take a minute to research the internet to figure out the average net profit real estate investors make per flip in your area. We are in Texas, and this was published in early 2023: "Profits vary by metro area and even from property to property. However, a flipper in Texas typically made around $43,000 to $62,000 per property in 2022."

Again, we had two properties with net profits of around $5,000 and a third property that made just under $10K in net profit. You may ask yourself if we thought of quitting or doing something else. The answer is no. Now, let us be clear: If every deal we flipped yielded this kind of profit, we would surely reconsider our answer. Fortunately, these are a minority, and other flips realized a six-figure profit.

With a growth and resilient mindset, the not-so-successful ventures can be seen as a learning experience—like getting paid to learn. While we haven't ever lost money on a deal, it is not that uncommon. One must be ready to count the losses if applicable, recover quickly, and move on to the next deal.

HVNLY Tip: "Beware of little expenses; a small leak will sink a great ship. -Benjamin Franklin

ALTERNATIVE AND ADVANCED INVESTMENT STRATEGIES

Traditional methods often lead to saturated markets. Alternative strategies, however, offer the chance to explore new potential and diversify. Vacation rentals are an exciting option. They tap into the trend of experiential travel and the shift toward homey accommodations over standard hotels. Driven by platforms like Airbnb and VRBO, vacation rentals have evolved into a profitable opportunity, drawing investors looking to make the most of this expanding market.

VACATION RENTALS: SHORT-TERM PROFITS IN DESIRABLE LOCATIONS

Market Research for High-Demand Areas

Choosing the best places for vacation rentals comes down to knowing about tourist trends, when people travel the most, and what makes an area unique. Popular places often have things in common, like being close to well-known sights, beautiful scenery, or fun places that bring in a stream of visitors. For example, if your location is near a national park open year-round, you're more likely to book it often. Tools like AirDNA can help you determine how often a place is booked, how much you can charge daily, and how much money you might make to find a rental that'll bring in good money.

Regulatory Considerations

The rules for vacation rentals vary depending on where you are. They can involve many things, like who can rent out the property and what taxes must be paid. Some places only let you rent out places in certain areas, and you might have to have special permits, make sure your place is safe, and pay local taxes. For example, a beach town famous for getaways might have rules on how many times you can rent out a place each year, which could affect how much money you make. To ensure you do everything right and avoid legal trouble, keep up with these rules by talking to local officials or getting legal advice.

Operational Strategies

Running a vacation rental requires keeping guests happy and ensuring things run smoothly. You'll need a good cleaning service that you can count on to keep the place spotless for each new visitor. It could also be helpful to have an easy booking process that works well with big rental websites to keep your place booked as much as possible. Using smart tech like code locks and internet-connected thermostats makes things easier for guests and lets owners handle stuff from afar. Managing a rental well usually means staying on top of things or working with a company that knows about vacation rentals. It's about finding the right balance between being in charge and making things easy.

Marketing Your Vacation Rental

With so many vacation rentals, making yours stand out is essential. A marketing plan can help you get there and use excellent photos and good descriptions of your place and its surrounding area. Social media can help show off what makes your rental special and the cool things to do nearby, and you can target the right people with ads. If you talk to people who've stayed previously, get them to write reviews, and answer questions fast, you'll build a reputation that'll bring repeat business and word-of-mouth referrals. Working with local businesses like cafes, restaurants, and people who run tours can help you put together special deals that make staying at your place even better while getting the word out to more people.

Vacation Rental Checklist

When you're thinking about getting into the vacation rental business, here are a few tips to keep you on track:

- Pick the Right Spot: Do your homework to find places where lots of tourists go and where there are fun things to do.
- Follow the Rules: Know the local rules, get necessary permits, and understand how taxes work.
- Get Organized: Have a system for cleaning, bookings, and keeping the place in good shape.
- Advertise Well: Use great photos and write-ups. Get the word out on social media and consider ways to keep guests returning.
- Money Matters: Calculate your expected earnings from bookings, daily charges, and costs to determine whether it's worth it.

Remember, it's all about being well-prepared and planning smart to maximize opportunities. Getting into vacation rentals is more than just earning quick cash in popular spots; you must study the market, play by the rules, know how to run things and promote your place.

Here's a link to one of the short-term rentals we own as a reference:

https://airbnb.com/h/bellavacationhome

MASTERING THE 1031 EXCHANGE FOR TAX DEFERMENT

Real estate investing offers excellent opportunities for making money and growing your investments. An intelligent investor knows how to delay paying taxes, especially with a 1031 exchange. Section 1031 of the U.S. Internal Revenue Code lets investors put off paying taxes on profits when they swap one property for another. This can help grow portfolios and build wealth over time. The key idea is that investors have a chance to move their money from one place to another without an immediate tax hit, adding up over time.

1031 Exchange Basics

The 1031 exchange is a tax strategy that lets investors delay paying taxes on profits from selling a property if they use those profits to buy a similar property. This is not a tax avoidance strategy; it's simply about putting taxes off for later. However, with specific guidelines, the new investment must be of the same or greater value than the old one.

This strategy can be used for all properties, whether they're for business or investment, which opens more opportunities—from empty land to office buildings.

Qualifying Properties

Choosing suitable properties for a 1031 exchange is vital because not all property sales qualify. To be eligible, the property must be used for business or as an investment, not for personal use or flips. Not paying attention to this rule can lead to having to pay taxes you didn't expect. For example, a rental property could qualify, but one you're fixing up to sell right away doesn't. It's essential to look at what properties you have and make sure your investment plan fits within the 1031 exchange rules.

Timelines and Rules

Pulling off a 1031 exchange means sticking to a tight schedule. Once you sell your property, the clock starts ticking. You have 45 days to pick out potential new properties that fit what you're looking for and meet the exchange rules. After you've made your choice, you have 180 days to complete the property purchase. There's no wiggle room here, so missing deadlines means losing out on tax benefits. So it's so important to plan carefully and act precisely.

Strategies for Maximizing Benefits

The 1031 exchange is a smart way to grow your investment portfolio. Savvy investors use each exchange to save on taxes but also to enhance their portfolio, moving money from less successful investments to ones that could earn more or bring variety by moving into new areas or properties. For example, someone could switch from renting houses to investing in office buildings. This could mean less risk and a chance at making more money. Or they might combine a few smaller properties into one big one, eliminating the hassle of managing several properties while still making good money.

The 1031 exchange allows investors to keep their money moving while avoiding upfront taxes. However, investors must have a sharp eye for suitable properties, follow strict timelines, and think ahead about portfolio management.

INVESTING IN REAL ESTATE INVESTMENT TRUSTS (REITS)

Real Estate Investment Trusts (REITs) are an exciting way for investors to get involved in real estate without owning property. They work by paying out most of their earnings to the people with shares in a trust, blending the easy-to-sell nature of stocks with the reliable income and stability of real estate.

REITs Explained

REITs were created to allow regular people to earn money from commercial real estate—something previously reserved for the rich. REITs pool cash from many investors to buy and own properties, like office buildings, shopping centers, and large apartment complexes that bring in regular income. The beauty of REITs is that they allow investors to get a cut of the rental income and any increase in property value without having to manage the property.

Types of REITs

There are different types of REITs. Equity REITs, which are the most common, use their money to own and run properties that make money, like offices or apartments, and the cash paid out to investors mainly comes from the rent they collect. Mortgage REITs (mREITs) lend money for real estate and make their cash from the interest paid on these loans. Hybrid REITs mix it up, holding properties and giving out loans, aiming for the steady earnings equity REITs provide, plus the high-income potential from the interest of mREITs. Each kind has its risks and rewards; equity REITs can provide a steady income and an opportunity to earn more if the property's value goes up, while mREITs offer higher earnings but are more sensitive to changes in interest rates, and hybrid REITs try to get the best of both worlds.

Analyzing REIT Performance

When seeing how well a REIT is doing, don't just look at how much it pays out in dividends. Consider a combination of factors that show if it's in good financial shape, how well it's being run, and how it stands in the market. The dividend yield can tell you about its money-making ability, but you should also check out the Net Asset Value (NAV). The NAV gives you the value of all the property the REIT owns, minus any debts, and is a good indicator of how well the REIT manages its assets and if it keeps dividends up over time. Then there's the total return, which combines the dividends plus any increase in the value of the REIT's shares. This gives you the complete picture of its profit-making ability, including how much money you get and how much the investment could grow. All these details provide a well-rounded view of a REIT's performance, helping to make intelligent investment choices.

REIT Investment Strategies

Adding REITs to your investment portfolio requires assessing your risk tolerance, liquidity needs, and long-term financial goals. If you're seeking steady cash flow, equity REITs that regularly pay good dividends, particularly in sectors with consistent demand like healthcare or housing, could be your best bet. On the other hand, if you're willing to take on more risk for potentially higher returns, certain REITs might be more attractive, especially when interest rates are low or falling.

Like with any investment, opting for different REIT types can protect you against ups and downs and allow you to grow with the real estate market. Also, since the real estate market goes through cycles, make sure you're keeping an eye on economic signs or changes in different property sectors and adjust your investments to align with market trends.

REITs offer investors the chance to get into real estate, which is usually hard to get into. They allow you to put your money into actual buildings and benefit from economic activity that keeps property values going. By understanding how REITs work and considering how they fit into your overall investment plan, you can tap into the income and growth they offer without having to manage the properties yourself.

SYNDICATION IN REAL ESTATE: POOLING RESOURCES FOR LARGER DEALS

Syndication Explained

Real estate syndication opens the door for investors to team up and put their money into giant real estate projects that would be too costly to take on independently. First, the syndicator is the person who knows how to invest, finds a suitable property and figures out how to profit from it. Next, they bring together various investors' funds to buy and manage the property. This allows more people to invest in pricey real estate by lowering the financial barriers that keep small investors out and is a game-changer. It will enable people to share in the benefits of owning property— the potential increase in value, the rent they can collect, and the tax benefits—all without having to manage the day-to-day.

Structuring a Syndicate

Setting up a successful real estate syndicate requires setting up a structure that considers everyone's interests and where all the rules are followed. Syndicates are often set up as limited partnerships (LPs) or limited liability companies (LLCs). The person leading the charge is known as the general partner or manager, and the investors come in as limited partners or members. This setup clarifies who does what and how money gets split up, ensuring investors get paid back based on what they put in.

The critical piece is having a solid operating agreement that covers how the syndicate is run, how and when money is distributed, and what happens if people want to leave. This is about making intelligent plans that help the investment thrive and keep risks low.

Finding and Vetting Syndication Opportunities

Doing the homework to find suitable real estate investments is almost as exciting as joining a syndicate. The syndicator must comb through properties to find the ones that could bring in a lot of money and fit the group's objectives. Using real estate data platforms and their network, they gather research to get the scoop on what's happening in the market, how much properties are worth, and where there might be an opportunity for growth. However, it's not all about profits; they must also look at all the risks, like market fluctuations, the condition of properties, and any rules that might change.

Managing Investor Relations

Real estate syndicates thrive on transparent, consistent communication between the syndicator and investors. This relationship, nurtured through regular updates, detailed reports, and open lines of communication, fosters trust and collaboration. Effective management of investor relations involves:

- Sharing successes and navigating challenges together.
- Providing insights into decision-making processes.
- Offering reassurances during downturns.

Investor tools like online portals are essential because they give up-to-date information on how the investment is doing, what's new with the properties, and what's happening in the market. These tools do a great job of keeping everyone in the loop. Plus, when investors are part of big decisions, it shows teamwork and reassures investors that they're helping steer the ship.

We have just covered two advanced strategies that allow investors to participate in real estate without being actively involved. When considering investments in REITs or real estate syndications, it is essential to understand the monetary requirements, including minimum investment amounts, fees, and liquidity. Publicly traded REITs generally offer lower barriers to entry and greater liquidity, while private REITs and syndications often require higher initial investments, more significant fees, and longer-term commitments.

MONETARY REQUIREMENTS TO PARTICIPATE IN A REAL ESTATE REIT OR SYNDICATION

Real Estate Investment Trusts (REITs)

1. Minimum Investment Amount:

- Publicly Traded REITs: Typically, the minimum investment is relatively low, similar to buying shares of any public company. Depending on the REIT, this could be as little as the cost of one share, ranging from $10 to several hundred dollars.
- Private REITs often require higher minimum investments, typically ranging from $1,000 to $25,000 or more.

2. Investment Fees:

- Public REITs may include brokerage fees for buying and selling shares, like any other stock transaction.
- Private REITs often have higher fees, including management fees, performance fees, and sometimes upfront sales charges.

3. Liquidity:

- Public REITs: Highly liquid, as they can be bought and sold on major stock exchanges.
- Private REITs: Less liquid, often requiring a more extended commitment period, and potentially difficult to sell quickly.

Real Estate Syndications

1. Minimum Investment Amount:

- The minimum investment for real estate syndications typically ranges from $25,000 to $100,000, but this amount can vary significantly depending on the syndication and the size of the project.

2. Investment Fees:

Syndications usually involve several types of fees:

- **Acquisition Fee:** A fee paid to the sponsor for finding, evaluating, and purchasing the property, typically 1-3% of the property's purchase price.
- **Asset Management Fee:** An ongoing property management fee, usually 1-2% of the gross income.
- **Disposition Fee:** A property selling fee, often around 1-2% of the sale price.
- **Performance Fee:** Also known as the "promote," a share of the profits above a certain threshold paid to the syndicator.

3. Accreditation Requirements:

Many syndications require investors to be accredited. To be an accredited investor, one must:

- Have an annual income of at least $200,000 (or $300,000 combined with a spouse) for the last two years, with the expectation of earning the same or higher in the current year.

- Have a net worth over $1 million, individually, or jointly with a spouse, excluding the value of the primary residence.

4. Liquidity:

- Real estate syndications are typically illiquid investments. Investors should be prepared to commit their capital for several years, usually 5-10 years, depending on the business plan of the syndication.

EXPLORING COMMERCIAL TO RESIDENTIAL CONVERSIONS

Turning commercial spaces into homes is a trend that's growing in popularity. It's all about adapting to how cities are changing and what people want from where they live. As cities and what residents expect from living spaces evolve, investors must be ready to take on the challenge and handle complicated rules and planning issues to find exciting opportunities to reshape properties.

Market Demand for Conversions

People are turning old commercial buildings into new homes for a few reasons. First, living in city centers is trendy, but there needs to be more space to build new homes. Plus, buildings with a cool, unique look are super attractive. These home makeovers are perfect for folks who want to be close to where they work, and all the city has to offer. More and more, people like the idea of living where neighborhoods feel alive and are accessible without a car.

To get it right, you must study what's going on with housing in the area, how fast the population is growing, and what specific groups of people are looking for in a home, making sure the changes you want to make are what people are looking for.

Challenges and Solutions

Turning old commercial buildings into new homes can be challenging. You've got to deal with strict rules about how buildings can be used, and you often need special permission to change a building's use. These can help:

- Talk to the city planning folks early to determine what you can do.
- Have a good plan that shows how your project will help the neighborhood.
- Get legal advice from experts who know how to work through the red tape.

Keep in mind that commercial spaces aren't built to be homes, so you'll need to do significant work to add kitchens, bathrooms, and cozy living areas. Work with experienced architects and engineers to ensure your new designs are innovative and safe.

Finding the money to make these changes can also be tricky since banks are often cautious about these types of projects. However, other ways exist to get funding, like investor groups, borrowing from non-traditional lenders, or using grants to help develop properties. If you can show that your plan is well-thought-out and could make money, you're more likely to get the funding you need to get started.

Case Studies

Looking at real-life examples of commercial spaces that have been turned into homes can teach us about what makes these projects work. Take, for instance, an old factory in our downtown area that was converted into trendy loft apartments. The people behind this project kept the relaxed factory vibe and used its old-school details to attract people looking for something different. In the Dallas downtown area, an office building in the city center was transformed into living spaces with shops on the ground floor. Thanks to intelligent planning and community engagement, they got the go-ahead to add more apartments in the building than usual. Having a clear vision, making intelligent plans, and involving the community can help you solve the kinks of turning old buildings into new homes.

Best Practices for Project Execution

Turning commercial spaces into residential areas requires careful planning and a clear vision. It starts by ensuring the project is possible by examining costs, the building's structure, and what people want. Bringing in a diverse group of experts early on, like designers, engineers, people who understand the city, and legal experts, helps plan well and tackle problems head-on.

It's super important to manage the project well by setting deadlines, monitoring the budget, and ensuring everything's done right. Keeping everyone in the loop is key to keeping things moving smoothly and building trust.

Nowadays, you also must think about the environment. Developers are using eco-friendly building methods and tech to create places that look good and are environmentally conscious, appealing to more buyers.

These projects are complex but rewarding, mixing deep market knowledge with creative problem-solving and working well with others. This journey can lead to investments that meet the needs of today's city life and personal tastes, showing off the real power of what real estate can do.

ADVANCED MARKET ANALYSIS TECHNIQUES FOR STRATEGIC INVESTMENTS

Real estate analysis has come a long way. This new era is defined by advanced analytics and AI, which give a detailed view of market trends and how to make intelligent investment moves.

Big data can help predict what's next. Packed with information from various sources like sales, shopping habits, and economic patterns, AI can predict market changes and pinpoint where the market is headed, giving investors a heads-up on where to look for opportunities.

But it's not all about tech. Understanding people's ages, earnings, jobs, and where they move helps too. Noticing that a town's demographics are changing might help you see that more rentals are needed. Or if average pay goes up, there could be more demand for excellent homes.

The real estate market swings with the economy—things like interest rates and jobs can signal its health. Then, there are significant shifts, like more people working from home or wanting greener living spaces, which change what kinds of properties are in demand. To stay ahead, look at both these short-term cycles and long-term changes.

Using advanced analytics in real estate means making decisions based on solid data. This new approach helps spot hidden opportunities, reduce risks, and place investments strategically for both the short and long term. With big data, AI predictions, and an understanding of demographic trends, you can make the best moves.

Building a Real Estate Portfolio with Limited Partnerships

Limited partnerships allow individual investors to come together, combine their strengths and resources, and tackle more significant real estate projects. These partnerships offer protection against personal loss if things get tough and intelligent tax benefits that help keep more profits in their pockets.

Limited partnerships are set up so that each person's risk is limited to what they've invested, which keeps personal assets safe. Plus, profits go straight to the investors without being taxed twice, and they can write off things like mortgage interest and other costs, making these deals even more appealing.

Starting a partnership means choosing your team carefully. Partners should share similar goals and be willing to take on similar levels of risk. You can find potential partners at networking events and through real estate groups. Once you've got your team, create an agreement that lays out how you'll split profits, who does what, and how you'll handle disagreements.

By having a team of investors, you can spread your money across different properties and areas. This spreads out the risk and adds variety to your investments, which can protect you when the market fluctuates.

Beyond purchasing property, running these investments well requires clear communication and meeting the group's goals. If disagreements pop up, handle them as you've agreed to. When it's time to sell or end the partnership, do so strategically to maximize everyone's returns and ensure a fair wrap-up.

Exploring alternative and advanced investment strategies can be promising. Each offers a path filled with opportunities for those who either choose to venture alone or are ready to join forces and navigate the market together.

HVNLY Tip: "If you have knowledge, let others light their candles in it."- Margaret Fuller

TAX STRATEGIES AND LEGAL CONSIDERATIONS FOR THE SAVVY INVESTOR

Experienced real estate investors use tax advantages and write-offs to find growth opportunities. Knowledge is power and can turn tax duties into opportunities for building wealth. However, we strongly recommend working with an accountant who knows the code and how it relates to real estate investment.

TAX BENEFITS AND DEDUCTIONS EVERY REAL ESTATE INVESTOR SHOULD KNOW

Identifying Deductible Expenses

Understanding IRS rules can lessen your tax responsibilities. Investors use legal deductions to increase their profits after taxes, which include mortgage interest. This is a big part of the cost and can be deducted if the loan is used to buy a building or to make significant improvements. This cut in taxable income means you owe less money to the IRS because you borrowed money to invest.

Property taxes paid on real estate are also fully deductible, offering an easy way to reduce taxable income. Then there are the everyday costs of running and fixing a property, like utility bills and paying for management—these expenses can be deducted immediately. However, the deduction must be spread over several years when you improve a property, not just fix it. It's a fine line between what counts as a repair, which you can write off immediately, and an improvement, which adds value over time and doesn't provide an immediate tax benefit.

Depreciation Benefits

Depreciation is the IRS' way of acknowledging that property wears over time. It's an excellent way for investors to account for the cost of the property used to make income. You can write off part of the property's value every year over what the IRS considers the property's "useful life." For example, if you own a rental house, you can spread this deduction over 27.5 years, lowering your taxable income yearly. By spreading out deductions over time, you can delay some of your tax payments, helping you to hold onto more cash. Without a doubt, depreciation is a fantastic way to build wealth in real estate.

Opportunity Zones

Opportunity Zones were introduced as part of the Tax Cuts and Jobs Act of 2017 and create tax perks to encourage people to inject money into places that need it. By investing through Qualified Opportunity Funds in designated areas, you can delay paying taxes on your profits, and if you keep your investment for over ten years, you could even avoid paying taxes indefinitely. This does more than give a tax break; it allows investors to help communities that could use a boost, making it beneficial for both the investor and the neighborhood.

1031 Exchange Revisited

The 1031 exchange was previously covered in Chapter 7 as an advanced investment strategy. It is mentioned once again as a savvy tax strategy for investors. It allows them to delay paying taxes on profits from a property sale if they reinvest that money into a similar property. Investors often use it as a chance to upgrade and add variety, essentially letting their investments grow over time without taking a tax hit. This is all about making smart choices to get the most out of the tax benefits available.

TAX DEDUCTION CHECKLIST

Before filing your taxes, run through this checklist to make sure that you haven't overlooked any deductions:

- **Mortgage Interest:** Verify interest expense on loans for acquiring, constructing, or improving properties.
- **Property Taxes:** Compile all property tax payments.
- **Operating Expenses:** List all costs incurred in property management, ensuring separate repairs from improvements.
- **Depreciation:** Calculate depreciation for each property based on the IRS schedule.
- **Opportunity Zone Investments:** Document investments in Qualified Opportunity Funds and their holding periods.
- **1031 Exchanges:** Track all properties acquired through 1031 exchanges, noting dates of sale and reinvestment.

This checklist can help you capture every available deduction and maximize the profitability of your real estate ventures. Yet, hiring the right CPA is highly recommended.

Structuring Your Investments for Tax Efficiency

Picking the proper legal structure is a big deal—it can make a huge difference in taxes and the safety of your investments. Selecting the right structure is critical, and understanding the difference between LLCs, S-Corps, and Limited Partnerships can help you make the best choice.

LLCs are common in real estate because they combine flexibility with protection. They offer pass-through taxation, so profits go straight to the owners without being taxed twice, and they protect your assets if there's trouble. S-Corps also let profits pass through, avoiding the double tax of regular corporations. They do set strict rules about who can be an owner and how to take money out, but they can save you on self-employment taxes if you get regular income from your investments.

Limited Partnerships are all about teamwork with clear roles. General partners run the show and face the risks, while limited partners invest and enjoy the profits without having to manage anything directly.

There's also the Qualified Business Income (QBI) deduction, which lets you reduce taxable income from a pass-through entity by up to 20%, but figuring out if you qualify can be tricky.

When it comes to borrowing money, the choices—like a traditional mortgage, a private loan, or other creative ways—each impact taxes. And for those investing in property overseas, the plot thickens with foreign tax credits and treaty benefits to consider.

This complex mix of tax strategies and legal structures creates both a challenge and an opportunity. Every choice, from how to set up your entity to how you fund your investments, is part of a larger plan to maximize tax benefits. It's about understanding taxes and being ready for what might change to make sure your investments grow.

LEGAL ENTITIES FOR REAL ESTATE: PROTECTING YOUR ASSETS

How well you understand and use legal structures can make the difference between just getting by and striking it big. Setting up your investment with the correct legal entity is critical to protecting it from risk and making the most of tax breaks. It requires you to use all the legal tools you have to keep your assets safe.

Asset Protection Strategies

Picking the proper legal structure is essential. Whether it's an LLC or a trust, each one offers protections against lawsuits and debts that could come knocking. Making this choice is a big part of your strategy, as it's about making things easier to manage and keeping risks under control.

Take LLCs, for instance. These keep your personal money and assets safe if your business gets into legal trouble or racks up debts. Trusts, especially land trusts in real estate, go even further by keeping your identity and connection to the property private, which adds another layer of protection. This way, any problems or debts tied to the property don't lead straight back to you. However, as always, we recommend consulting a tax expert.

Operational Compliance

Real estate investing isn't just about picking the right property; it's about staying on the right side of the law. This means paying close attention to all the rules—from ensuring you're fair in who you rent to and keeping the environment in mind. Doing things right from the start can save you from big headaches later.

You should never wait for problems to appear; you should get ahead of them. Ensure your property management is up to scratch and keep an eye on things like following fair housing laws and ensuring buildings are up to code. Also, consider the environment when buying a new property to avoid issues with land use down the road.

Staying compliant is an ongoing job that requires you to adapt to changing laws. The goal is to spot issues before they become serious problems that could cost you.

Anonymity and Privacy

With so much information just a click away, keeping your investments private is more important than ever. That's where trusts and LLCs come in. Not only do they protect you if things go wrong, but they also help keep your name out of the spotlight.

Using these legal setups means setting up your business so that the company's name appears on all the paperwork rather than your own. Put your properties in a trust that an LLC runs so that if someone tries to track you down, they'll hit a dead end. These tactics add extra layers of security that help protect both your money and your privacy.

Cross-Entity Strategies

When protecting your investments, use legal entities to spread properties across different LLCs so that each owns just one property. This way, if something goes wrong with one, the problems don't spread to the others. Some investors set up a holding company, set up as an S-Corp because of the tax perks, to oversee everything. Others use Trusts, ensuring their wealth goes where they want it to.

Setting these structures up provides a strong shield that keeps your assets safe now and sets up your financial future. It's complex, but getting it right means your real estate investments can weather just about any storm, from lawsuits to taxes, and stand the test of time.

NAVIGATING ZONING LAWS AND REGULATIONS

Understanding Zoning Laws

Zoning laws decide what and where you can build. Think of them like a board game, where each type of building has its spot. Some areas are for houses, some are for shops, and others might be for factories.

Before you buy land to build something, you need to know what the zoning laws say you can do with it. These laws tell you how big your building can be, how high it can be, and what you can use it for. Understanding these rules is important because they can change what you can do with your property and how much it's worth.

Pay close attention to these zoning laws so you know the rules before deciding on what properties to buy and what you can do with them. You'll also need to follow additional rules that dictate how much space you need to leave open around buildings, where people can park, and take care of the environment.

Variances and Rezoning

Sometimes, investors find a piece of land they think could be worth more if they transform it into something different than current zoning laws allow. This is where 'variances' and 'rezoning' come into play.

A 'variance' is like asking for special permission to bend the rules slightly. For example, you may want to build taller than the law usually allows or closer to the street. It would help if you convinced the local zoning board that your plan works and won't bother the neighbors or the town.

'Rezoning' is a bigger deal. Here, you're looking to completely change the type of buildings allowed on your piece of land. If you get it right, you can make the land much more valuable—like changing an old parking lot into a new shopping center. But this isn't easy. You must gather facts to support your case, talk with people living nearby to get them on board and show the town leaders that your idea fits their plans.

Both these steps can be tricky, but knowing who to talk to, what to say, and how to work with the community to turn your ideas into reality can help.

Impact on Investment Strategy

Zoning laws govern the rules for building in a city. They tell you what you can create and where. These laws are crucial because they can make a piece of land more or less valuable, depending on what you can do.

Look at these rules before you buy land. Have plans in place that fit these rules or find ways to alter them slightly. Sometimes, you might ask for a 'variance' for a rule to be somewhat bent for their project. Other times, you might need something more significant, like 'rezoning.' This means you want to change the rules for what can be built, making the land more valuable. But it takes work; it involves lots of paperwork, talking to neighbors, and convincing city officials.

Consider these zoning rules and how they might change. If the zoning laws change, some pieces of land become much more valuable, but it's not always a sure thing, and it takes work to make the changes happen.

Staying Informed and Compliant

Understanding and following zoning laws is a must-do for real estate investors. To stay on top of things:

- Watch what the city or town planners do so you're never caught off guard by new rules.
- Talk with the local planning offices, getting the latest updates directly from the source.
- Get to know the people who enforce zoning laws, which can make everything smoother.

It's hard work, but it can help you avoid surprises. Zoning laws can both limit and open up opportunities in real estate. Finding new opportunities for success takes planning, not simply waiting around for changes to happen but making them happen yourself.

ESTATE PLANNING AND REAL ESTATE: SECURING YOUR LEGACY

Understanding the importance of estate planning for your investments is crucial in securing your family's future. Real estate often represents a significant portion of people's wealth, and by planning effectively, you can ensure it becomes a legacy for your loved ones. A well-crafted estate plan not only preserves the value of your properties but also safeguards your family from substantial tax burdens.

Follow these steps to make this happen:

- **Use trusts to protect your property:** Think of trusts like special containers for your real estate that come with instructions. You decide how and when your family gets to use the property, and you might even save them from dealing with taxes and court processes. Trusts are flexible; you can change one if you need to (like living trusts) or lock them in (like irrevocable trusts).
- **Make a game plan:** If you're part of a real estate business or partnership, you need to think about who will take over and how to keep things running without hiccups. Set a clear plan for who will take charge and how the business will continue making money.

Remember, Estate planning isn't just about leaving your family property; it's about empowering them with knowledge and responsibility. Early involvement in decision-making and gradual ownership transfer can be beneficial, not just for family dynamics but also for tax planning. By doing so, you can secure your family's success and future.

When investing in real estate, you're not just accumulating assets; you're building a legacy. You're weaving together estate planning, using trusts effectively, preparing for business succession, and carefully managing wealth transfer. You're creating a legacy of responsibility, vision, and family growth. This way, your investment does more than grow in value; it becomes the foundation for your family's future successes.

Integrating real estate into your estate planning is critical. Through strategic estate planning, you can protect your assets, control who manages them and when, and plan for taxes and inheritance in a way that sets your family up for success for generations to come.

HVNLY Tip: "When prosperity comes, do not use all of it."
~Confucius~

SUSTAINING GROWTH TO ENSURE FINANCIAL FREEDOM

This chapter will discuss how to ensure sustained growth, from emotional intelligence and adopting sustainable/green practices to technological advancements and creating a personalized real estate investment plan.

Even in real estate, where it's all about numbers, being smart about people's feelings and why they act the way they do (that's emotional intelligence) is essential. You've got to understand what others are feeling and why they do things, especially when making a deal.

THE ROLE OF EMOTIONAL INTELLIGENCE IN REAL ESTATE NEGOTIATIONS

Understanding Emotional Intelligence

Emotional intelligence is about understanding feelings—both yours and other people's—and using that understanding to get along and work together better. In real estate, where making deals is a big part of the job, having good emotional intelligence will help you manage tough conversations, find what people care about, and keep calm when things get heated.

Imagine you're trying to buy a house from someone who is very attached to it. They might need help talking through selling it. Your emotional intelligence enables you to understand how hard this might be for them. Take the time to listen and show that you understand it's not just a simple business deal. This can help you make an offer they feel good about while ensuring the deal works for you.

Reading Situations and People

Being able to read people and situations is a big part of what makes you better equipped to handle feelings in business. In real estate deals, you must consider what people say and how they say it. The way someone pauses can show they're not sure, a change in their voice might mean they have worries they're not disclosing, or a bit of excitement might mean they're ready to find a middle ground.

Empathy and Rapport

Being able to understand and share someone else's feelings—empathy is super important when making a deal. In real estate, buying and selling homes is a big deal for people, and it is often more personal than it is about money. You can turn a tense negotiation into a team effort when you show that you get how another person feels.

How? By listening to what they're saying, showing that you take their views seriously, and sometimes sharing your own stories to show that you understand and have been in a similar spot. This can help everyone feel like they're on the same side and make it easier to work out a deal.

Negotiation Tactics

To negotiate well, especially in real estate, you must strike a balance between sticking to your guns and being open to change. You need to be able to fight for what you want but also listen and give the other person's point of view credit. Ask intelligent questions that make the other person think differently but in a way that doesn't make them defensive. You can also try giving a little on your end first—like throwing in something extra or being willing to bend a bit. This can make the other person want to work with you and maybe give a little back, too.

Sample Guidelines for Negotiating Tactics in Real Estate for a Win-Win Outcome

Negotiating a real estate deal effectively involves strategies that ensure both the buyer and seller feel they have achieved a favorable outcome. Here are the best guidelines for achieving a win-win negotiation:

Preparation is Key

- **Market Research:** Understand current market conditions, including comparable property sales, trends, and neighborhood data. This knowledge will help you justify your offer and counteroffers.
- **Know Your Limits:** Be clear on your budget, financing options, and what you're willing to compromise on. Having a pre-approval letter can strengthen your position.
- **Understand the Seller's Motivations:** Knowing why the seller is selling (e.g., downsizing, relocation, financial reasons) can help tailor your offer to meet their needs.

Build Rapport and Trust

- **Positive Communication:** Establish a good relationship with the seller or their agent. Be respectful, professional, and open in your communication.
- **Find Common Ground:** Look for shared interests or goals to help build connections and foster a cooperative atmosphere.

Create Value Through Terms, Not Just Price

- **Flexible Terms:** Be open to negotiating terms such as the closing date, repairs, and inclusions/exclusions of personal property. Sometimes, flexibility on these points can lead to a better overall deal.
- **Win-Win Solutions:** Propose solutions that benefit both parties. For example, offer a quick closing date if the seller is in a hurry or suggest lease-back options if they need more time to move.

Use Strategic Offers and Counteroffers

- **Start with a Reasonable Offer:** Begin with an offer that is lower than your maximum budget but within a reasonable range. This shows you are serious but still leaves room for negotiation.
- **Counteroffer Wisely:** Respond to counteroffers promptly and with thoughtful adjustments that reflect both parties' needs and market realities.

Leverage Contingencies Carefully

- **Inspection Contingency:** Ensure your offer includes an inspection contingency to allow for property evaluation. Use the inspection results to negotiate repairs or price adjustments.
- **Financing Contingency:** Include a financing contingency to protect yourself in case your loan approval falls through.

Maintain Flexibility and Patience

- **Stay Calm:** Keep emotions in check and remain patient throughout the negotiation process. Avoid making hasty decisions under pressure.
- **Be Ready to Walk Away:** Know when to walk away if the deal does not meet your essential criteria. Sometimes, the best negotiation tactic is showing that you have other options.

Close the Deal with Clear Communication

- **Summarize Agreement:** Once an agreement is reached, summarize the terms to ensure both parties are on the same page.
- **Professional Help:** Use a real estate attorney or experienced agent to review all documents and contracts to ensure everything is legally sound.

Post-Negotiation Follow-Up

- **Check-in:** After closing, follow up with the seller to ensure all agreed-upon conditions are met. This helps maintain goodwill and can be helpful for future transactions or referrals.

Emotional Intelligence Reflection Questions

Getting better at understanding feelings means asking yourself some critical questions after you finish a deal:

- What feelings did I pick up from the other person, and how did those feelings affect the deal?
- Did I keep calm when things heated, or did we disagree?
- What body language did I notice, and what could it tell me about what the other person was thinking?
- How did I show I understood their feelings, and how did that change how things went?
- What strategies did I use during negotiations, and how did I use emotional smarts to decide on those?

These questions can help you improve your ability to read the room and handle your emotions, which will make you a better negotiator. In this business, where numbers meet nerves, being good with emotions is a must. It helps you turn tough negotiations into smoother conversations, turn rivals into teammates, and close deals.

ADOPTING SUSTAINABLE AND GREEN INVESTING PRACTICES

Today, being eco-friendly is a big deal. Even if this is not your cup of tea or a subject of interest, it is something you need to know about. People are increasingly looking to invest in properties that are good for the planet and can make the properties worth more in the long run. It's clear now that taking care of the environment doesn't just feel good—it can also be good for your wallet, as green buildings attract more buyers and renters who care about healthy and sustainable living.

Benefits of Green Investments

Green investments are becoming popular because they benefit the planet and make sense financially. Many are looking for buildings that save energy, cut down on pollution, and give people a healthier place to live. These places often rent or sell faster and can charge more for rent.

Investors are paying attention to these changes and are starting to measure a property's worth based on its greenness. The government is also making it easier to invest in green buildings by offering tax breaks. These perks make it a smart move for your conscience and bank account.

Implementing Sustainable Practices

Shifting to green property management means being more eco-friendly, which is good for the planet and your business. Here's how it's done:

- Start by using energy-saving lights and heating/cooling systems to reduce power use and save money.

- Install water-saving toilets and showers, collect rainwater to use less water, and lower the water bill.
- Use eco-friendly cleaning products and maintenance practices to keep living spaces healthy and green.

These make properties more attractive and help keep the costs of running them down.

Eco-Friendly Building Materials and Technologies

Going green in property development is all about choosing materials and tech that are kind to the environment. For example, you could build using recycled steel for the structure, bamboo for the floors, and paint that doesn't give off harmful fumes. These options use sustainable materials that are recyclable or that come from sources we can keep using, like bamboo.

Adding smart tech helps, too. Things like thermostats, systems that monitor a building's energy use, and solar panels can reduce energy use. This is great for the environment and saves money over time.

CERTIFICATIONS AND STANDARDS

Green investing is all about meeting specific standards that show a building is eco-friendly. A building can earn special badges like LEED, ENERGY STAR, and BREEAM. These badges are a big deal because they tell people that the building saves energy and is built with mindfulness. Earning eco-friendly badges also means you can benefit from any new green rules the government puts in place. Focus on green practices and do your part for the planet while setting yourself up for success in a more eco-aware world.

The Impact of Technological Advancements on Real Estate

Technology is changing the game in real estate investment. Fundamental tools like artificial intelligence (AI), blockchain, and the Internet of Things (IoT) are being used today. These tech advancements are shaking things up, changing how deals are done, how properties are managed, and how the market is understood. They're making everything faster and more intelligent and creating new ways to make money in real estate.

Emerging Technologies

As discussed previously, Artificial intelligence (AI) allows investors to use data to make better investment choices and spot new trends. AI can analyze tons of information about prices, people, and the economy to predict what might happen next, helping investors see the future more clearly and giving renters precisely what they want.

Blockchain is also changing real estate deals by making everything more open and secure. It can keep track of property records in a way that can't be changed, making the whole process more transparent and quicker. It also lets people own parts of real estate, making investing possible for more people.

The Internet of Things (IoT) connects devices, making them more innovative and efficient. Smart thermostats and leak detectors help save energy, keep places safe, and improve living standards while keeping buildings greener and more eco-friendly.

PropTech for Efficiency and Growth

PropTech is a fancy term for using technology to improve real estate. New tools help with everything from managing buildings and finding tenants to figuring out the best ways to use space and handle money. With intelligent software, investors can check out the market, spot good places to put their money, and make sure they're offering what people want.

This tech makes things run smoother. It helps tenants and property managers communicate more easily online. They can sign leases, pay rent, or request repairs with just a few clicks, keeping tenants happier. And happy tenants are more likely to stay, which translates to reliable income for property owners and, in the end, buildings that are worth more.

Virtual and Augmented Reality

Virtual and augmented reality are changing how people tour and customize properties without being there in person. Virtual tours use 360-degree videos and VR headsets to give potential buyers or renters a feel of a place, no matter where or what time it is. This can help them make decisions faster without having to visit the property.

AR also allows people to use their phones or AR glasses to see what a furnished property would look like, with different layouts or new wall colors. It makes looking at the property more fun and helps people see it as their own future home.

Technology as a Competitive Advantage

Embracing AI, blockchain, and IoT makes everything smoother and keeps tenants happy. Tech also means you can base your choices on solid data, not just guesswork, making investments less risky and opening new chances to make money.

These new tools help with property management and make the renting or buying experience better for everyone.

PREPARING FOR MARKET FLUCTUATIONS: A RESILIENT INVESTOR'S GUIDE

Real Estate Market Cycles Simplified: Imagine the real estate market as a big wheel that keeps turning. This wheel goes through four cycles, just like seasons in a year:

- Expansion: Everything's growing, buildings are popping up, and more people want to buy properties.
- Peak: The top-of-the-market - properties are at their most expensive, and it seems things can't get any better.
- Contraction: Things start cooling off - fewer people are buying, and prices stop climbing.
- Trough: The lowest point - people aren't investing much, and things are a bit gloomy.

Reading the Signs:

You must pay attention to the clues to know what part of the cycle we're in.

- Employment: More jobs usually mean more people looking for homes.
- Interest Rates: High rates can slow buying because loans are pricier.
- New Builds: Lots of construction often means a growing market.

These hints help you guess what the market will do next.

Playing it Smart:

How to play it smart:

- Spread Your Bets: Don't put all your money in one place. Own different kinds of properties across several locations.
- Save for Rainy Days: Keep some cash handy. That way, when the market dips, you won't have to sell in a panic and can even afford to buy more if prices drop.
- Be Ready to Move: Markets change, so be ready to change your strategy. If things are tight, invest in cheaper housing or convert a shopping center into apartments.
- Choose Wisely: Pick properties that people will always need in places that are always popular and keep them in good shape.
- Go Green and Smart: Properties that save energy or have smart tech can save you money and attract tenants.

Thriving Through Ups and Downs: It's about planning, being flexible, and making choices that last through good times and bad. It's about surviving the market's ups and downs and doing well because you're prepared.

CREATING A PERSONALIZED REAL ESTATE INVESTMENT PLAN

Crafting Your Investment Blueprint:

1. **Define Your Financial Destination:** Identify what you want to achieve with your investments. Set specific and ambitious goals yet within reach. Reflect on:

- What are your financial targets?
- What level of risk are you comfortable with?

- What is your investment time horizon?

Your answers will shape your investment strategy and help keep you on track.

Note: You might still be wondering how you will get started with no money, no credit, no real estate contacts, and no idea how to start building your team. So, here's some valuable advice:

Get information about local REIAs in your town to start networking. This will help you develop the right mindset—one of success, positivity, and abundance.

Join podcasts like Bigger Pockets to embark on a journey of learning. They will inspire you and provide valuable insights on what to do and what not to do.

If you are looking to build reserves, look to the wholesaling method. Whether you're looking to flip, start a short-term rental, house hack, or explore the BRRRR method, choose wisely. Your options might be limited based on your area or current market conditions.

If you are still unclear on the difference between working for a paycheck and letting your investments/assets work for you, read books like Rich Dad and Poor Dad.

Take charge of your financial future by building your credit. Whether you're starting from scratch or need to restore your score, remember that the higher your credit score, the better the terms you'll be offered. Work towards achieving an 800+ credit score, knowing that you're taking a significant step towards financial empowerment.

2. Select Your Investment Pathways: With clear goals, explore the different ways to invest. This could include:

- Buying property directly.
- Investing in Real Estate Investment Trusts (REITs).
- Participating in real estate crowdfunding opportunities.

Evaluate each option based on how quickly you need returns, your comfort with market fluctuations, and how soon you need to access your funds.

3. Conduct Regular Portfolio Assessments: The property market can shift, so it's crucial to take responsibility for your investments and periodically review them. This will help you see if your portfolio is performing as expected or adjust if necessary.

4. Seek Knowledge and Advice: Remember, you're not alone in this journey. Consulting with experienced investors can offer valuable perspectives and help refine your strategy. Choose mentors who are reputable and offer tangible benefits. Focus on ongoing education by staying up to date on market trends and expanding your knowledge.

5. Implement and Adapt: When you're ready to proceed with a solid plan that's based on your individual goals and preferences and equipped with expert advice, be prepared to adapt your strategies as you gain experience and market conditions evolve.

Scaling Your Real Estate Investments: Strategies for Portfolio Expansion

Growing in real estate isn't just about buying more properties. It's about intelligent planning, taking risks carefully, and thinking ahead. You need to know when to add to your investments and how to do it wisely.

Strategic Scaling

Growing your real estate investments is a big move that requires good timing, having enough money, matching your long-term plans, and comfort with risk. Expanding when you spot opportunities and looking for undervalued markets also helps. It's also important to look at what you already own, sell things that will earn a little more, and use that money for new opportunities. This will help you diversify your investments and boost your earnings.

Diversification Across Markets

Lowering risk is about spreading out your choices. You should mix up locations, types of properties, and the kinds of tenants you have. Being in different markets with economic ups and downs makes your investments safer if one area has trouble. Balance your investments to keep things stable through market changes and turn risks into chances for even growth.

Leveraging Equity and Cash Flow

To boost property investments, you can tap into the equity of what you already own. Equity grows as property prices rise and mortgages shrink. You can access it with a refinance or a line of credit, buying more without selling. However, overborrowing can be risky, so using debt smartly is critical.

At the same time, make your existing properties work harder for you. This means streamlining operations, tweaking rent prices, or making upgrades that increase property value. Using your equity wisely and maximizing property income can help grow your portfolio and keep it resilient, even in tough economic times.

Building Your Team

To grow your investment portfolio, you must assemble a team of real estate professionals that you can count on. From the person who might help you to find a deal, such as a realtor or a wholesaler, to the closing on the property at a title company and everything in between, such as the loan officer and property inspector, every person in that team is extremely valuable. Building lasting relationships with your team and being a repeat customer with them is worth your time and effort.

Furthermore, if you choose to rehab properties, be it to flip or to hold as rentals, the most prominent team by your side is the one that works in your properties day in and day out to realize the rehabs. It is because of those people that the projects get done. In our company, we are the general contractor and keep our team of carpenters, tiler-setters, drywall-setters, and painters working from project to project and providing maintenance to our rentals. We make sure they know that they are the backbone of our company and, most importantly, that they feel appreciated for it.

Success isn't just about expanding; it's about growing wisely, exploring various markets, leveraging your assets, and having a trustworthy crew. Focus on these aspects, and success will follow.

HVNLY Tip: Don't be afraid to give up the good to go for the great.— John D. Rockefeller

OUR STORY - THE NITTY GRITTY

Our story, Raquenel and Norma's story, began over 25 years ago. After meeting by chance in 1997, we have been best friends, female entrepreneurs, and business partners ever since. We are both minorities, and English is a second language for one of us and a third language for the other. We are also both divorced, have children, and come from entrepreneurial parents. So, it's safe to say that we are similar in many ways.

A FRIENDSHIP WORTH A FORTUNE

Raquenel comes from parents who, after losing everything in a business venture and having to live off welfare, had the opportunity to turn the big house they lived in into several small apartments. Having experienced firsthand what it is to struggle and how real estate can help was the beautiful beginning of her journey toward financial independence.

Norma comes from a business-minded family. Her grandparents, aunts, uncles, cousins, parents, and siblings all have businesses and work for themselves. Having learned what it takes to run a business and how profitable it can be, she has followed in their footsteps and has owned all types of businesses, from preschools to real estate assets.

A Business Partnership Meant to Be

When we met, Norma owned a preschool program licensed for 35 children. Years passed, and in 2003, an opportunity to open a second, more extensive preschool presented itself. This location was licensed for 143 children, and while we were nervous about the big purchase, it was a very exciting time. We decided that we could purchase and run it successfully if we partnered up. Yet, there was so much to consider and so many financial details to figure out that the venture seemed daunting. But together, we felt it was the right choice, so we went all in and decided to move forward with acquiring the new center.

Although Raquenel had home-schooled her children, her college degree had nothing to do with education, which added to her nervousness. Running a preschool program was new to her, so she decided to return to school to succeed in her new role as administrator of an educational system. Norma would continue to serve as program director at Tots R Us, a role she was willing and prepared to continue fulfilling. She told Raquenel, "There is no way we're going to buy a school together where the teachers and director know more than you." The business was bought, and A+ Child's Galaxy Academic Development Services was created.

The Good, the Bad & the Ugly

We mentioned this business, A+ Child's Galaxy, in Chapter 3's Case Study regarding creative financing. Although you did get a rundown of how things went, we did not get into the many ups and downs, financial hardships, and lack of sleep it took to take that asset from a $750K valuation to one of $1.25M within three years. By no means are we mentioning this to discourage you from pursuing similar ventures, but we want to make sure that we are as transparent as we can be about our journey. And the truth is, it took tremendous time, effort, sweat, and tears to grow that business. Fortunately, we had each other, but not even that was comforting at times.

As previously mentioned, we purchased this school under an SBA loan program, and if you are familiar with these types of loans, you know that they tend to be scrutinized for approval. Qualifying for an SBA loan is not for the faint of heart. We needed to come up with a $75,000 down payment for the closing; Norma's condo qualified for an equity line of credit. Some of you might think, "Who in their right mind would jeopardize their home for a business venture? What if things didn't go as planned?" To be honest, it was a tough decision to make. But we were both very invested. We will say that it takes a very positive and growth mindset to make a decision like this.

The school was privately advertised among brokers with an enrollment of 66 children, but as fate and life would have it, there were only 12 children in the program and five staff members on payroll the day of closing. Talk about deception and fraud; there we were, faced with feelings of hopelessness and defeat. We contacted a lawyer, but there was little that could be done. Building a case and taking it to court could take months, if not years, and legal expenses were not a luxury that we could afford at the time.

Stressful days, weeks, and months followed as we chose not to let go of the staff on payroll and worked tirelessly to make the program grow. We implemented every strategy we could think of to try and expand the program. A van was bought to pick up children from the neighboring elementary schools, bring them to the afterschool program, and help them complete homework. We would take our own kids out on the weekends to pass out flyers advertising our afterschool program. During this time, there was absolutely nothing glamorous about being a business owner, just dedication and a desire to succeed. Not giving up took courage, discipline, and a strong abundance mindset.

For almost two years, Norma's original preschool, Tots R Us, covered the losses of the new program, A+ Child's Galaxy. During this time, Raquenel worried, cried, and hoped for the day that our accounting books weren't in the red anymore. It seemed like Norma had risked her condo for a business with little hope, which had every indication of failure. Yet Norma managed to stay positive and hopeful and always had encouraging words for those around her. She constantly reassured everyone, "Everything is going to be alright." Thankfully, one partner remained optimistic and was able to calm the other, no matter the situation. One day, seemingly out of nowhere, a ray of sunshine beamed down on the program, and hope for transformation was on the horizon.

Without even knowing who she was talking to, Raquenel connected with someone who held an influential position in the public sector and was directly involved in early childhood funding programs. This angel informed us about several grants available to qualifying programs in certain targeted zones. Fortunately, our program was a candidate, but there was a catch: we'd have to write a winning grant proposal. This opportunity seemed far-fetched for two people who knew nothing about grant writing.

For the next several weeks, Raquenel invested as much time as possible in writing a grant proposal that we hoped would dig us out of the hole we felt we were in. The grant proposal was submitted, and by some miracle, our program was awarded the grant. Consequently, the school flourished, and many children were able to benefit from this turn of events. And, as they say, the rest of the story is history. But, still, from time to time, we wonder if it was some divine intervention or simply a by-product of the effort and dedication we put in. We like to think it was a combination of the two. And finally, the days of tears and heartache became a thing of the past. We were able to sell the school and use the money we made for our next endeavor, real estate.

REAL ESTATE INVESTING ON THE HORIZON

Life happened, and we both ended up moving to Texas, where we started investing. Our real estate journey began in 2007, buying foreclosed houses in cash from the city's courthouse. Later, we figured out that we could purchase these foreclosures online, bought some owner-financed properties, and even used a traditional bank with 3% down. Everything was going well; we fixed these properties well, remodeled them to be the nicest on the block, and placed them for rent. We took all the proceeds from our school's sale and invested them in real estate — We went all in. We remained motivated to try new things, which eventually led to new, profitable, and not-so-profitable ventures.

We learned about forex exchange and online trading and paid for mentorship, realizing that education was the only way to get where we wanted. Unfortunately, our trading venture ended in disaster because we were stubborn. This was an important lesson for us, which we've discussed throughout the book: the importance of knowing your stuff and following the rules and procedures set in place. We made a lot of money but lost even more of it. Once again, Norma had nothing but encouraging words, "We make the money; money does not make us," "Everything is going to be alright." Sound familiar?

We were invited to visit Panama to assist and mentor teaching staff there. Norma taught teaching methodology and classroom environment arrangement for the school's preschool program that would soon be opening. After this experience, we realized we missed owning a preschool. In an attempt to recoup the $150K+ lost in forex trading, we decided to start searching and planning to purchase a new school. However, we needed cash to make this new business plan a reality.

Often, time goes round and round and brings us opportunities we should be ready to capture and benefit from. The real estate asset (a block of apartments) that had once set Raquenel's parents financially free would now serve as collateral for the purchase of the property we'd eventually transform into a small private school program. And just like that, Thomas Jefferson Schoolhouse was born in 2010.

This educational program ran for six years, transforming many children's lives and building beautiful and lasting relationships with parents that still hold to this day. As life would have it, Raquenel got sick with shingles, which led to a long-term sensitivity to sound. Afterward, dealing with children's natural noise levels became something she couldn't tolerate. She knew she wouldn't be able to continue in this field, knowing that the quality of her work could be compromised due to her lingering condition. Norma was unwilling to run the program on her own, so together, they continued to run the school as things got sorted out and the school year ended.

Norma reluctantly agreed to close the educational program but refused to sell the real estate. Eventually, we decided to transform the building into a rental property that could accommodate college students with an all-utilities paid and fully furnished setup. We were both very excited about this new venture. Thomas Jefferson Schoolhouse closed its doors in June 2016, and we began advertising rooms for rent later that year. This creative transformation allowed us to start earning significant passive income, and soon, we were making more than we'd been earning by being physically present and running our educational program. To this day, it remains the most significant passive income source in our rental portfolio.

Moving forward, we focused on building a passive income through rental acquisitions until 2020, when COVID-19 happened. Up until then, we kept our business very private and personal. Once again, we pursued online education and mentorship and started flipping properties and living the HGTV dream. We've developed a successful flipping business with a public profile that we're proud of.

Living the Dream

Earlier in the book, we mentioned the advantages of networking, building meaningful relationships, and learning from one another.

Along the way, we were blessed to meet incredible humans who freely and selflessly shared their knowledge with us. We were introduced to the BRRRR method, and whether it was an act of God, a gift from above, or everything lining up in our favor, we were able to take advantage of low interest rates and reasonably priced homes poised for value-add. Please note that while we are not currently in that real estate market cycle, it is important to realize that the market is cyclical. This is the time to prepare and be ready to take advantage of the next "generous" cycle that will come our way!

We focused on buying properties at 70% of ARV (After Repair Value) minus repairs, carefully working rehab numbers to ensure our success. We followed the 1% rule for rentals, where the costs (purchase plus rehab) add up to 1% of the monthly rent. Here is a sample description of this combination investment strategy. While the numbers and percentages are not set in stone, staying within the range will ensure success.

THE BLENDED FORMULA TO OUR PORTFOLIO SUCCESS

Understanding 70% ARV Minus Repairs

ARV (After Repair Value): The estimated value of a property after all necessary repairs and renovations are completed.

70% Rule: This is a guideline used by real estate investors to determine the maximum purchase price of a property. According to this rule, investors should pay no more than 70% of the ARV minus the estimated repair costs.

Example:

- **ARV:** $200,000
- **Estimated Repair Costs:** $30,000

- **Calculation:** $200,000 x 0.70 = $140,000 - $30,000 = $110,000

In this example, the maximum price you should pay for the property is $110,000.

Implementing the 1% Rule for Rentals

1% Rule: This rental property guideline suggests that the monthly rent should be at least 1% of the property's purchase price plus repairs to ensure positive cash flow.

Example:

- **Purchase Price:** $110,000
- **Repairs:** $30,000
- **Calculation:** $110,000 + $30,000 = $140,000 x (.01) = $1,400

This means the property should rent for at least $1,400 per month.

Combining Both Strategies

When combining the 70% ARV rule with the 1% rule, you ensure that you buy properties at a discount, allowing room for repair costs and potential profit while also ensuring that the property will generate sufficient rental income to cover expenses and provide a positive cash flow.

Scenario:

- **ARV:** $200,000
- **Estimated Repair Costs:** $30,000
- **Maximum Purchase Price:** $110,000
- **Required Monthly Rent:** $1,400

By purchasing the property at $110,000 and ensuring it can rent for at least $1,400 per month, you adhere to both investment strategies, positioning yourself for profitability.

Benefits of This Approach:

- **Risk Mitigation:** By purchasing below market value, you create a buffer against market fluctuations.
- **Cash Flow:** Ensuring the property meets the 1% rule helps maintain positive cash flow, covering mortgage payments, maintenance, and other expenses.
- **Equity Growth:** Buying at a discount increases equity once repairs are completed and the property is valued at the ARV.

This combined approach of purchasing real estate at 70% ARV minus repairs and using the 1% rule for rentals is a powerful strategy for maximizing returns and ensuring positive cash flow. It helps investors manage risks and achieve long-term financial success in real estate investing.

Having the right numbers is important, and finding the right property often feels like we are looking for a needle in a haystack. So, we are cautious and don't jump at any deal that comes our way. We were and continue to be very selective and believe more than anything that it is not about quantity but quality.

Our portfolio has grown exponentially, and our net worth has grown alongside it. We have achieved the financial freedom many people so earnestly seek and can honestly say we're living our best lives. We share our story to speak our truth and in hopes of encouraging others to pursue real estate. If we did it, you can too!

The secret to success includes minding one's mindset, credit, spending, willingness to learn from others, dedication, discipline, humility to receive advice, endurance, relationships, resilience, and vision. Has it been easy? It depends on how you define it. We know it is not for everyone, but if you are passionate about it, go for it. If you're on the fence, jump.

HVNLY Tip: Whether you think you can or think you can't, you're right.– Henry Ford

SHARE YOUR REVIEW AND HELP FELLOW INVESTORS!

We hope you're enjoying "The Art of Creative Real Estate Investing" by HVNLY Publishing. Your journey towards financial freedom is just beginning, and your feedback can make a big difference.

How You Can Help:

• **Share Your Experience:** What did you love about the book? Did a specific chapter or tip stand out and help you?

• **Keep It Simple:** A few sentences about what you liked and how the book helped you is perfect.

• **Be Honest:** Your genuine opinion helps us improve and guide other readers.

Why It Matters: Your review is crucial. It helps others decide if this book is right for them and enables us to create better content for future investors like you.

Thank you for being part of our community and helping us make this book the best it can be!

Happy Investing!

Scan the QR code to leave a review.

CONCLUSION

As we wrap up this comprehensive guide on creative real estate investing, we want to return to the main idea that inspired this journey. This book is about making real estate investing clear and doable for everyone. Whether you're starting or aiming to grow a big portfolio, this guide has your back. It's packed with insights to help you step into the investing world with confidence, no matter your budget or background.

We've gone over the basics, from getting the hang of the market to understanding creative financing, and even covered the BRRRR method. We've looked into making money by flipping properties and examined less common investment options that break the mold and open up new chances for success.

But let's remember, investing is about more than making money. It's about doing it in a way that's good for the community and the world at large. Real estate investing should be positive all around, promoting sustainability and leaving a mark of honesty and honor.

Investing in real estate is powerful and a catalyst for personal transformation. Beyond building wealth, it's about reaching for your dreams, growing as a person, and leading a life that's full of purpose and joy. This book gives you a plan not just for investing success but for achieving a future where you're truly free and deeply fulfilled.

Now it's your turn to take that brave first step on your own real estate adventure. Armed with the knowledge from this book, you're ready to make intelligent choices. Real estate is varied and constantly changing, full of chances for everyone, no matter your starting point.

Remember, real estate investing is dynamic, constantly evolving with new trends and technologies. The key to staying ahead is to remain informed and adaptable. This guide encourages you to keep learning and growing, equipping you with the tools to navigate the ever-changing real estate world.

Dive into the community of investors beyond this book. Join discussions, attend events, and connect with peers. Sharing your stories and lessons is priceless, creating a network of support and collective insight.

Thank you for letting us guide you toward your investment goals. The ideas we've talked about have been crucial in our own financial journey, and we hope they'll help you build your wealth and reach your dreams.

 Let's go forward, creating wealth and legacy rich in knowledge, power, and lasting achievement. Welcome to the thrilling world of creative real estate investing—your adventure starts right now.

TOOLS, TEMPLATES & DIGITAL RESOURCES

https://rb.gy/ebhnsa (Bigger Pockets Rental Property Calculator)

https://www.calculator.net/roi-calculator.html (ROI Calculator)

https://www.fortunebuilders.com/real-estate-calculator/ (10 RE Calculators Every Investor Should Know)

Financial Models and Spreadsheets

Vertex42 and *Template.net* offer templates for real estate financial models that include cash flow projections, ROI calculations, and rental property income statements.

Smartsheet provides customizable templates for real estate financial analysis, helping you calculate returns, expenses, and profitability.

Business Plans for Real Estate Investing

Bplans and *Template.net* feature business plan templates specifically designed for real estate investments. These can guide you through setting up your investment goals, strategy, market analysis, and financial projections.

Real Estate Marketing Templates

Canva and *Adobe Spark* offer a wide range of design templates for marketing real estate properties, including brochures, flyers, and social media posts, which are essential for presenting properties to potential investors and tenants.

Lease Agreements and Other Legal Documents

LawDepot and *Rocket Lawyer* provide customizable templates for lease agreements, purchase agreements, and other legal documents needed in real estate transactions.

Property Management Templates

Template Archive and *Smartsheet* offer templates for property management tasks such as tenant background checks, maintenance requests, and rent collection.

REFERENCES

Real Estate Investment: 20 Must-Know Terms for Beginners https://longleaflending.com/real-estate-investment-terms

Understanding Property Law in International Real Estate. https://www.anna.realestate/post/understanding-property-law-in-international-real-estate

How Important Is Your Credit Score In Real Estate? https://www.fortunebuilders.com/how-important-is-your-credit-score-in-real-estate/

The Ins and Outs of Seller-Financed Real Estate Deals https://www.investopedia.com/articles/mortgages-real-estate/10/should-you-use-seller-financing.asp

Best Real Estate Crowdfunding Platforms Of April 2024 https://www.forbes.com/advisor/investing/best-real-estate-crowdfunding-platforms/

Case Study: My BRRRR (Buy, Rehab, Rent, Refinance, Repeat) Success—All In Under 75% ARV https://www.biggerpockets.com/blog/brrrr-success

How to Do a Real Estate Market Analysis https://realwealth.com/learn/how-to-do-a-real-estate-market-analysis/

7 Tips To Budget For Renovations https://www.century21wright.com/client-articles/2023/12/14/7-tips-to-budget-for-renovations#:~:

The Complete Guide to Tenant Screening https://www.avail.co/education/guides/complete-guide-to-tenant-screening

Real Estate Success Stories: Inspiring Journeys of ... https://www.linkedin.com/pulse/real-estate-success-stories-inspiring-journeys

9 Proven Networking Tips for Real Estate Agents https://www.realvolve.com/blog/9-proven-networking-tips-for-real-estate-agents/

Top 10 Real Estate Investor Software for Managing Rentals https://www.doorloop.com/blog/real-estate-investor-software

7 Legal Considerations Every Real Estate Investor Should Know https://trinh.law/7-legal-considerations-every-real-estate-investor-should-know/

What Is The 70% Rule In House Flipping? https://www.rocketmortgage.com/learn/what-is-70-rule-in-house-flipping

Creative Financing for Real Estate (14 Options for Investors) https://www.biggerpockets.com/blog/creative-financing

How to Plan Your Rehab Project Timelines When Flipping ... https://www.flipperforce.com/how-to-flip-houses/managing-your-rehab-project/rehab-project-timeline

51 Real Estate Marketing Strategies: Ideas, Tools & Plans ... https://www.iovox.com/blog/real-estate-marketing

United States Vacation Rental Market Report 2023-2026 ... https://finance.yahoo.com/news/united-states-vacation-rental-market-105800884.html

Top 4 Commercial Real Estate Investment Strategies [2024] https://www.investopedia.com/financial-edge/0110/10-things-to-know-about-1031-exchanges.aspx

5 Types of REITs and How to Invest in Them https://www.investopedia.com/articles/mortgages-real-estate/10/real-estate-investment-trust-reit.asp

Land Development Process In 6 Steps https://goodegginvestments.com/blog/a-behind-the-scenes-look-at-3-multifamily-real-estate-syndications/

Publication 530 (2023), Tax Information for Homeowners https://www.irs.gov/publications/p530

1031 Exchange: What Real Estate Investors Need To Know https://www.rocketmortgage.com/learn/1031-exchange

LLC vs. S-Corp for Real Estate: Which Business Model ... https://www.azibo.com/blog/llc-vs-s-corp-for-real-estate

Estate Planning for Real Estate Investors & Property Owners https://www.jpmorgan.com/insights/real-estate/commercial-real-estate/estate-planning-commercial-real-estate

Emotional Intelligence as a Negotiating Skill https://www.pon.harvard.edu/daily/negotiation-skills-daily/the-limits-of-emotional-intelligence-as-a-negotiation-skill/

How to create value through sustainability in real estate https://www.pwc.com/us/en/industries/financial-services/library/sustainable-real-estate-initiatives.html

Incorporating Proptech Into Commercial Real Estate - Forbes https://www.forbes.com/sites/forbesbusinesscouncil/2024/01/02/incorporating-proptech-into-commercial-real-estate/

Understanding the Four Phases of the Real Estate Cycle https://www.gripinvest.in/blog/real-estate-market-cycles-timing-strategies